CONCILIUM

D1711035

CONCILIUM 2005/2

HUNGER, BREAD AND EUCHARIST

Edited by
Christophe Boureux, Janet Martin Soskice and
Luiz Carlos Susin

SCM Press · London

Published by SCM Press, 9–17 St Albans Place, London N1 0NX

Copyright © Stichting Concilium

English translations copyright © 2005 SCM-Canterbury Press Ltd

ISBN 0 334 03083 8

Printed by William Clowes, Beccles, Suffolk

Concilium Published February, April, June, October
December

Contents

Introduction:
Hunger, Bread and Eucharist

CHRISTOPHE BOUREUX, JANET MARTIN SOSKICE AND
LUIZ CARLOS SUSIN

Hunger provokes the first and most basic movement of all animals and is, according to Emmanuel Levinas, the first impulse of the human being towards happiness – in the enjoyment of food. The hunger of an infant provides the outline of desire, and is desire in its most primordial and genuine form. The hunger of the infant also attests to the precarious dependence of every living being on an other who, in their turn, must search for and receive food. Thus hunger reveals to us our first relationship and becomes a metaphor for all the others, including the relationship of the human creature to the Creator and Giver of bread.

Bread, the biblical 'food', is at the same the most material, most bodily and most spiritual thing in Christian spirituality. The Eucharist, the mystery of faith, is bread. For this reason the sacrament is also a sign of our social nature, of the search for and the giving of bread – the mouth of the infant, the mother's breast – and sign of the most primordial forms of justice and of gift.

Too much hunger, too many mouths and not enough bread: this situation reveals the menacing nearness of death. The fact is that in our world many know the pains of a hunger that will not be satisfied. This opens the space for the Eucharist as a celebration of hunger, desire and the Bread given by God, but only if the Eucharist itself is involved in the struggle for justice. All this means that in our world, the same world as that of Jesus but one in which bread does not multiply but hunger in fact does, the Eucharist and justice are joined together.

Hunger is not only for bread. Augustine, speaking in his *Confessions* to God of an experience at Milan before his final conversion, says 'I seemed to hear your voice from on high: 'I am the food of the mature; grow then, and you will eat me. You will not change me into yourself like bodily food: you will be changed into me.' (*Confessions*, VII. 10.16). This is the Christian hope, but this hope for spiritual feeding and Love of God cannot, as Augustine repeatedly said, be separated from love of neighbour. and proper love of self. From the earliest Christian writings it has always been possible to focus to exclusively on spiritual hunger to the cost of the actual poor, or to do the reverse. The best of Christian reflection has held both together, and we have tried to do so here in a collection that touches on social and political action, biblical interpretation, historical theology, philosophy, spirituality and pastoral care. We hope the readers will be nourished by it.

1. Hunger Today

Zero Hunger:
An Ethical-Political Project

FREI BETTO

On 12 December 2002, twenty days before the inauguration of Luiz Inácio Lula da Silva as President of Brazil, representatives of dozens of religious denominations (Christians, Jews, Muslims, those of African descent and others) gathered in São Paulo to give a positive response to the proposal launched by Lula on the day of his election: 'Zero Hunger', a great national joint endeavour to eradicate the destitution of 53 million Brazilians, or 11.4 million families.

The religious leaders signed the commitment to act as partners in the Zero Hunger project, in view of the fact that, 'hunger results from injustice and represents an offence against the Creator, since life is the greatest gift of God. We wish to provide our people with the means of eating healthily, in order to preserve the health of people and of the earth.' They took on the public commitment to 'mobilize all the faithful and followers of our religious denominations in support of this campaign that aims to ensure that those who are going hungry have access to food and also to social inclusion, through an educational process that avoids patronising and guarantees its beneficiaries dignity and citizenship', aware of the fact that, 'as religious tradition teaches, one cannot expect those who suffer hunger to practise the virtues. But it is also our concern, as religious leaders, to open the ways of access to Transcendence to all those who hunger for the spiritual life. We believe that to share bread is to share God.'

On 20 September 2004, at the United Nations headquarters in New York, Lula invited the nations of the world to undertake an urgent campaign against hunger. He was endorsed by fifty-six heads of state, including Pope John Paul II, represented there by Cardinal Angelo Sodano. George W. Bush was not one of these.

I have said many times that Zero Hunger is the political version of the multiplication of loaves and fishes carried out by Jesus to feed the hungry crowd. Those who share bread, share God. This is why Jesus taught us to pray 'Our Father' and for 'our daily bread'. To make bread something not just for ourselves, but for everyone, since he came 'that they may have life, and have it abundantly' (John 10.10).

According to the FAO, 831 million people are now living in a chronic state of malnutrition. Every day, 24,000 die of hunger, including a child under five years of age every minute. Why is it that there are so many campaigns around other causes of premature death, such as cancer, accidents, war and terrorism, without the same being true of hunger, which produces many more victims than these? I can think of only one explanation, and that is a cynical one: that, unlike those other causes, hunger is a respecter of class. It is as though we, the well fed, were saying, 'Let the wretched die of hunger; it doesn't affect us.'

Yet there is a growing appreciation of the fact that hunger is a scourge that needs urgent eradication. We need to engage ourselves in an effort to make poverty, like slavery and torture, be seen as a heinous crime, a serious violation of human rights.

Brazil's President Lula suffered from hunger in his childhood. Of the twelve children borne by his mother, four died prematurely from malnutrition. The history of Brazil, disfigured by 358 years of slavery, shows that a social problem begins to be solved only when it becomes a political question. This is what Lula is doing with hunger, placing it on Brazil's political agenda through the Zero Hunger project, and on the world's agenda through his participation in international bodies, such as the speech he made at the opening session of the UN General Assembly in September 2004, echoing the FAO's call for a 'World Alliance against Hunger'.

Zero Hunger in Brazil now benefits almost eight million families that have a monthly income of less than $100 (US). Since its launch in January 2003 the programme has been subjected to much groundless criticism. Many people imagined a vast gymkhana of food distribution, with thousands of lorries pouring out of Rio or São Paulo to take food to the poor of the North East, the poorest region of Brazil. But Zero Hunger is not a plan for direct aid of this sort. Its aims are social inclusion, access to work, achievement of citizenship and self-esteem.

All the families that benefit, of whom the government has a record, receive a sum each month of $73, paid directly to the woman for her to buy food, plus $15 for each child of school age. They are all bound to keep their children in school, to teach illiterate adults to read, and to keep up to date with the health programme for parents and children. This amounts to a considerable injection of resources each month, which serve to re-activate local economies. Local authorities become the focus of a whole set of public policies: literacy campaigns, health promotion, family farm improvement, individual and community kitchen-gardens, small loans, house building, and so on. The Zero Hunger programme has an accompanying 'Zero Thirst': the project of building one million cisterns to collect rainwater over the next five years, monitored by the ASA (Articulation of Semi-arid Regions) agency.

President Lula stresses the importance of the whole of society participating in the Zero Hunger project. Businesses, churches and other religious bodies, schools, NGOs, unions, trade associations and international agencies have all responded favourably to his appeal. In his effort to combat hunger and poverty in the world, in fulfilment of the Millennium Goals, Lula hopes the rest of the world will avoid what he has managed to avoid in Brazil – the attempt to combat hunger simply by distributing food. If rich countries send tons of food to the poorest parts of the world, they are guilty of four mistakes: they justify their agricultural subsidies; they destroy local cultures; they increase dependence on benefactors; and they encourage the corrupt politicians who will distribute the food. In Latin America we only have to look at the failure of the Alliance for Progress in the 1960s and that of the Green Revolution in the following decade to know what routes not to take.

The aim is to mobilize world resources, under UN supervision, in order to finance entrepreneurial schemes, co-operative movements, and sustainable development in the poorest regions. Hunger cannot be fought just through donations, or even by transfer of funds. These need to be complemented by effective policies of structural change, such as agrarian and fiscal reforms that are capable of lessening the concentration of income from land and financial dealings. And all this has to be guaranteed by a daring policy of loans and credit offered to the beneficiary families, who must become the target of an intense educational programme, so that they can become socio-economic units and active agents in political and historical processes.

'I was hungry and you gave me to eat', said Jesus incarnate in the figure of the poor. Fighting hunger is a gospel demand, an ethical imperative, a duty of citizenship and solidarity, so that we may be able to drag humankind out of the pre-history in which billions of people still cannot be sure of the most basic animal right – to eat.

Translated by Paul Burns

Further information at: www.fomezero.gov.br; www.fomezero.org.br; www.mobilizacao.org.br; escolasirmas@yahoo.com.br.

Divine Alimentation: Gastroeroticism and Eucharistic Desire

ANGEL F. MENDEZ

In the fall of 1972 the journal *Deadalus* published an exquisite essay by the Mexican writer Octavio Paz entitled 'Eroticism and Gastrosophy'[1] In this essay Paz echoes the central idea of Charles Fourier's *Le Nouveau Monde Amoureux*, that eroticism and gastrosophy (the love for food and gastronomy) are the most fundamental pleasures of human life. The former is the most intense, and the latter is the most extended. For Paz these two forms of pleasure are ultimately related to the reality of desire itself, a desire that 'simultaneously reveals to us what we are and beckons us to transcend ourselves in order to become the *others*.'[2] Paz describes desire as 'the active agent, the secret producer of changes, whether it be the passage from one flavor to another, or the contrast among flavors and textures. Desire, both in Gastronomy and Erotica, initiates a movement among substances, the bodies, and the sensations. It is the force that regulates connections, mixtures, and transmutations.'[3] Paz argues that eroticism is not (as for George Bataille) transgression, but representation. Eroticism is invention and envisioning in its desire for the other. Paz' connection of eroticism and gastrosophy in the act of desiring incarnates in the reality of the body and the senses where humans endlessly continue re-inventing themselves. And here Paz, linking eroticism and gastrosophy in the act of desiring, can be read as actually *incarnating* the reality of desire in the sensuality of the flesh, where human bodies endlessly re-invent themselves spiritually in a touch and taste that is beyond touching and tasting. In this union of the erotic and food love is also being re-imagined and re-enacted, for love, like gastrosophy and eroticism is a communion and collectivity that lifts the senses and the body toward spiritual perfection.

What I find most remarkable about Paz' essay is the way in which he connects eroticism and gastronomy, the body and the senses, and love and communion. For some readers, his view might seem exotic. And yet, when we look closely at the meaning and reality of the Eucharist, it seems to me that these extravagant elements are incredibly –if not miraculously— harmonized. Ultimately, what takes place in the Eucharist is a dynamics of desire: both God's desire to share divinity with humanity as well as humanity's desire for God. In the Eucharist, desire is the active agent in our relationship with God and with one another. And in this Eucharistic reality desire is not abstract –it is incarnate. Here our food is the body of Christ and our drink is his blood, and this through the materiality of bread and wine. In eating this divine food, sensuality –particularly the sense of taste—is paradoxically intensified in its materiality in a way that nothing material is left behind. Further, this act of participating in the Eucharist becomes transformation into the body of Christ, into an erotic/agapic community which is called to feed both physical and spiritual hungers. And to a certain extent (as Paz describes it) by this erotic and gastronomic act of the Eucharist, the self becomes the other. And yet, in the Eucharistic feast there is a step that moves beyond Paz' favoring of otherness and overcoming of the self. In the Eucharist the self is transfigured by the other but never becomes totally alien to her own self since she re-discovers a deeper reality of who she is, and through such a re-discovery she realizes that the other is intrinsic to her own configuration and self-constitution. In the Eucharist, self and other are no longer juxtaposed but mutually constituted. The Eucharist *is* communion: with God and with one another. In a way, the Eucharist reveals to us a more extravagant reality than that of Paz' envisioning: for here, in the eucharistic feast, God's excessive love feeds all our longing for God in a manner that satiation fills us with a desire to taste more of God-self, to have in our mouth what is still yet-to-come. And this erotic movement forward enkindles—and never diminishes—our desire for God, making us feasting pilgrims within history moving toward the *eschaton*: the final and total partaking of God's superabundant banquet.

I would like to take Paz' connection of eroticism and gastrosophy and explore it from the angle of a theology of the Eucharist. My main goal will be briefly to demonstrate that this connection between the erotic and the act of eating is indeed extravagant, for it is rooted on God's extravagant and excessive love as it is shared in the Trinitarian exchange of gifts. Such an extravagancy is further shared in creation, incarnation, and even more radically so in the eucharistic banquet whereby the act of eating and drinking Christ's body and blood becomes the medium of our deification, and thus the point of ecstatic union between humanity and God. I would like to construct the term 'gastroeroticism' in order to speak of the existing connection between the realities of self and other, the erotic and food, the material and the spiritual, the human and the divine. In this way gastroeroticism will be here re-figured as a theological term that is constructed from the perspective of a eucharistic discourse. The gastroeroticism that takes place in the Eucharist is not a mere aesthetic act. I will argue that both the aesthetic and the ethic realities complement one another in the Eucharist, and thus challenge us to look back to and transform our own world of hunger, exclusion, and violence.

Hunger, Desire, and the Gift as Alimentation

We are hungry beings. We are in eating, for without eating we perish. 'To be human is to be hungry. Not to be hungry is to be dead.'[4] There is 'another' when we eat: the concrete other than 'me'. This other is bread, food, is another person. We crave the other. Our cravings propel the drive of desiring. The root of eroticism is this desiring an-other-than-me, a desire to unite, ecstatically, with the other. We hunger for communion with others. But does this suggest that the root of all desiring is a fundamental (extended not only to an existential but even to an ontological level) lack?

By the logic of the Christian narrative, the root of all desire is not –as Graham Ward correctly explains—a lack, but the excessive sharing of love as it is envisioned in the Trinitarian community:

> Our inclination to crave the other, what Augustine would term our fundamental *appetitus*, is an image of the divine appetite in which the Father craves the Son and the Son the Father, and both the Spirit who maintains the eternal craving open with respect to the world God created out of this excess loving.[5]

From the perspective of the Christian narrative, God is envisioned as the perfect community of love. John D. Zizioulas argues that the practice of the Trinitarian community reveals that '[the] being of God is a relational being: without the concept of communion it would not be possible to speak of the being of God'.[6] God is communion, a Triune God who exists in an ecstatic loving-relationship of self-giving between Father, Son, and Holy Spirit and who invites us to be participants of God's perfect community of love.[7] The dynamics of this intra-Trinitarian community could be imagined as a dance, a perichoretic celebration of God's love for God. In this intra-Trinitarian perichoresis, suppression of difference into a centralized sameness never takes place, because it is precisely in sharing-difference that the rhythm and dynamics of this one perpetual flow beyond unity dances. This imagery of the Trinitarian dance of love evokes the infinite dynamics of God's offering to otherness the self-gift of love for the other, while simultaneously receiving the givenness of the other's love; and such an ecstatic reciprocity prevents self-annihilation by virtue of its relatedness, witnessing, and perpetual blessing of a third – the Holy Spirit. The exchange of the gift in the Trinitarian community is both excess and reciprocity, and it does not occur outside of, or prior to, its being given, received, and shared.[8]

This narrative tells us that 'something is cooking' in God. The Trinity establishes a movement of reciprocity that ultimately points toward an intra-Trinitarian movement of *desire* (Father for Son, and Son for Father), *preparation* (Spirit beatifying the Son), and *consumption* (union of Son within Father). Boldly speaking in line with these reflections, one could possibly expand the imagery in order to say that within God, there is a dynamic of alimentation: as God's intra-Trinitarian infinite self-*nourishing* which, by virtue of the economy of exchange and reciprocal relation of 'divine food-as-love', provides self-sustenance, co-existence, co-operation, and inner-vitality. Because God loves God, God desires God, God feeds God. God's desire does not go unfulfilled, but with the infinite generosity of divine food of Love, Truth, Beauty, and Goodness, God is abundantly nourishing as much as delighting in God-self. Herein, in God's Trinitarian movement of desire and alimentation, is founded a theology of gastroeroticism which is the precedent and true source of nourishment that we claim to receive in the Eucharist.

Here again, something needs to be said about the nature and constitution of desire and gastroeroticism within the erotic/agapeic community of the Trinity. For the vision of gift as alimentation shared in this triune community of God-self posits desire, not a lack, but as radical excess. In God, there is fulfillment and superabundance (alimentation) of desire in the reception of the gift; but there is always a desire for more, since God's Infinity (as the infinite givenness of God in love) anticipates the excessiveness that brings new dimensions to desiring. From this Trinitarian perspective, the gift is simultaneously consumption and desire, alimentation and preparation.

This Trinitarian agapeic/erotic dimension of the gift is further shared with all creation. Creation is a sign that points to the divine Creator, which implies that it is a sign that is not empty but participatory: it is a sign alimented by divine nourishment. Creation is like a cosmic banquet that expresses a delightful divine utterance that aliments in giving life and Being to all that 'is'. The psalmist enjoins us to 'taste and see the goodness of the Lord' (Psalm 34.8). This means to know creation as itself a series of 'edible' signs that are tasty, that taste of God, and so delightfully participate in the superabundance of God. And if creation is a *corpus* embraced and nourished by the infinite divine food of Love, Truth, Beauty, and Goodness, the creation is a cosmic banquet, and God is the perfect chef.

Eucharistic nourishment and sharing

Gastroeroticism comes to its most extravagant manifestation in the reality of the Eucharist, where Christ (the God-human) becomes food for us. Christ, the *Logos* of God, takes flesh in Jesus. And this incarnational gesture is in fact the ground and possibility of gift reception and gift-exchange. God incarnates and becomes human in order to share this love in human words and deeds, even to the point of death, which for the Christian faith, manifests a radical solidarity and non-indifference to humanity, particularly toward those suffering in our midst. Christians believe in the resurrection of Christ as the central manifestation of God's ever faithful covenant to humanity, which endures and rejoices in the message that love is stronger than death, that by love the Creator transgresses the boundary between creature and Creator and heals the wound of death. Christ's ascension into heaven opens an upward movement that dignifies and divinizes our human condition while promising a future deeper sharing and unity at the end of times. Christ is this ever living Trinitarian Word of Love who is nourishment for the whole human person. God is as God gives, and this giving is nourishing. The paradigm of kenosis of the gift is here taken from the Trinity, particularly as it is expressed in the incarnation of the *Logos* and then, in its most extravagant form of self-presencing, in its becoming food. The *Logos* performs an act of dispossession not as making self-sacrifice an end in itself but – from the context of the resurrection and of the Eucharist – as a practice of nourishment, hope, and trust for a return in God's superabundant love and fidelity.[9] And this practice is our deification.

The Eucharist is an extravagant form of divine alimentation. For Christianity, the Eucharistic banquet is the paradigm *par excellence* of the bridge between God and humanity. Through the Eucharist, God reveals a new and more plentiful sense of self-presence: God is both absent but also *wholly* present, not merely transcendent but immanent as well. This unique modality of presence in the Eucharist, wherein absence and presence are mutually constituted, reveals a new and quite 'extreme' mode of signification.[10] Through the Eucharist, God becomes food, a banquet to the senses, so that the believers can enter into an exchange of true intimacy with God and with one another. The gastroeroticism implicit in the act of eating is here intensified, for through the tasting and eating the precious body of Christ our somatic experience of the divine becomes the actual medium and guidance to our intellect and soul of an intimate ecstatic union with the divine.[11] The tasting of the divine in the Eucharist becomes a foretaste of the beatific vision. Thus, our partaking of this banquet, allows us to grasp reality in new and transformed ways, for our own senses, 'our fleshliness, and the contours of our thinking' are transfigured into the already trans-figured reality of creation: so that, 'in the reception of a world transfigured as a New Creation, perception is redeemed'.[12]

This way of seeing the world as a 'divine body' inaugurates the space of the Church as a Eucharistic community, which is 'a new kind of human embodiedness, one which is celebratory, Eucharistic and compassionate, and which discovers itself to be joyfully and limitlessly at one with the world-text's ceaseless play'.[13] The world as a divine body is eucharistic, it is a community that presents self and other as not mutually excluding, nor mutually lacking of their supposed counter-part. In this new kind of human embodiedness self and other are mutually constituting and complimenting without annihilating difference but making difference even more attractive and desirable. Here what is emphasized is not difference as such, but being-in-relation and co-participation. And, because of their (self and other) participating of God's excess, their desire for one another and for God per-petually increases as it moves forward into the culmination of history: the promise of perfect communion as a state of eternal ecstasy.

The Eucharist is the ecclesial performance and celebration of the gift of God's most intimate presence. But more, as communion, the Eucharist is transformative, and so calls us to be people of God through communion with God on the one hand, and also with the world, and most urgently toward those who hunger for bread, justice, and love. The kenotic act of the eucharistic gift performs a reversal and a paradoxical mode of alimentation. While we tend to think of food as becoming part of us or of our bodies when we eat, in the Eucharist we are reversely transformed and incorporated into the body of Christ. Kenosis is transfiguration, for now in eating Christ's body and blood, we become Eucharistic people, and are challenged to perform kenotic acts of true *caritas* with our brothers and sisters.

Through the sacramental gift of the Eucharist the Church participates in the superabundant economy that already takes place within the Trinity, and in turn engages in a process of preparation and nourishment: God, through the Son and in the Spirit, is the food of the world; the world, in the Spirit and through the Son, is the food of God. In the Eucharist God feeds creatures with God's very self. The Church is the community of believers who proclaim and live this message day by day throughout this itinerancy of history. This Eucharistic community from past, present, and future proclaims itself to be guided by the dynamic presence of the Holy Spirit that sustains and renews the individual and communal participation in God's banquet of love.

Conclusion

The communal practice of the Eucharist brings us back to our contingencies, situatedness, and embodiment, only to provide the possibility of being nourished by the plenitude of God's inexhaustible gift, and thus re-energize/re-generate the daily erotic/agapic exchange with God and one another.[14] The gastroeroticism that the Eucharist enacts is, then, a not merely aesthetic enactment, but it implies the ethical as well–the communal practice of the Good.

In a movement back to our own practices we are confronted by the reality of God's superabundance and generosity in the face of the world's reality. If God is nourishment, the theologian must urge humanity to eradicate both physical and spiritual hungers of the world. If God is superabundance, the theologian must ask how the world's wealth is distributed, and how it does or does not reflect God's generous sharing. If God is love, the theologian must speak against violence, exclusion, and destruction. The eucharistic community – whether priestly or lay, theologian or not – is the embodiment of divine alimentation and forever challenges us to look Eucharistically at our daily exchanges. Stephen Long poses some pertinent questions:

> How do we commute to and forth to work? What do such practices bear witness to? Do we treat creation merely as something to be consumed by our will, or can we find in it God's beauty? How do we eat? How are we clothed? What relationship exists between our eating, being clothed, and other people's lives? Can we avoid desire for its own sake, even if such avoidance is not necessarily good for economic growth?[15]

To be sure, the litany of questions that might be raised is inexhaustible. But most urgently, when our desire/hunger for God's *caritas* is lost . . . we starve to death.[16]

Notes

1. Octavio Paz, 'Eroticism and Gastrosophy', *Deadalus* (1972), pp. 67–85
2. Paz, 'Eroticism', p.74.
3. Paz, 'Eroticism', p.75.
4. Monica K. Hellwig, *The Eucharist and the Hunger of the World,* Wisconsin, Sheed and Ward, 1992, p. 3.
5. Graham Ward, *Cities of God*, London, Routledge, 2000, p. 172. Italics are from the text.
6. John D. Zizioulas, *Being as Communion: Studies on Personhood and the Church* (Crestwood, N.Y.: St. Vladimir's Seminary Press, 2002), p.17.
7. Oliver Davies explains this intra-Trinitarian exchange as a 'semiotic movement' of mutual interpretation and self-giving: 'The Word must in some sense give itself utterly to be interpreted or exegeted by the Father with the Spirit, and by the Spirit with the Father, and must itself exegete the Father with the Spirit, and the Spirit with the Father, in a continuous and infinite perichoresis of knowing and understanding through love and self-giving.' I am indebted to Oliver Davies for providing me with a copy of his forthcoming publication, *On the Creativity of God* (it will appear at the CUP Cambridge Studies in Christian Doctrine). Reference to this work will follow Davies' own copy which numbers pages as units/chapters. This quotation is from chapter 6, pages 1–2 (6: 1–2).
8. This summarized version of the gift is mainly taken from discussions with John Milbank during his teaching a doctoral seminar at the University of Virginia which was entitled 'French Modern Theology' (Spring 2003), and from the following of his works: 'Only Theology Overcomes Metaphysics' in *The Word Made Strange: Theology, Language, and Culture*, Oxford, Blackwell Publishers, 1997, pp. 36–52; 'Can the Gift Be Given?' *Modern Theology* (1995) 2:1, pp. 119–61; and 'The Soul of Reciprocity. Part I: Reciprocity Refused' *Modern Theology* (2001) 17:3, pp. 335–91; and finally, his most recent book, *Being Reconciled: Ontology and Pardon*, New York, Routledge, 2003.
9. This theology is comparable to the Gospel's discourse on the *Beatitudes*, where the gift is both kenosis and plenitude as it reveals the essential character of blessedness in the practice of dispossession *for* the other.
10. As Davies explains this sense of presence as not being ordinary, but it is rather 'a presence which is simultaneously an absence. Neither bread nor wine nor the body and blood are present on the altar in any ordinary sense, but both are present and absent in a reciprocal sense'. *On the Creativity of God*, 6:15.
11. A great source of inspiration for this paper, particularly regarding the subject of our deification through our bodies and sensual experience in the Eucharist feasting comes from John Milbank's and Catherine Pickstock's *Truth in Aquinas*, London, Routledge, 2001. This book also solidly argues in favor of a Christian understanding of desire not as a lack, but as plenitude.
12. Davies, *On the Creativity of God*, 6:16.

13. Davies, *On the Creativity of God*, 6:17.

14. See, for instance, Catherine Pickstock's brilliant reflection on the Eucharist where she also claims that desire in Christianity is understood not as 'absence, lack and perpetual postponement; [but] rather, desire as the free flow of actualization, perpetually renewed and never foreclosed'. As she argues, this desire brings us back to our bodies and communal practices. In 'Thomas Aquinas and the Quest for the Eucharist' *Modern Theology* (1999) 15:2, pp. 159–180. Here, 179.

15. D. Stephen Long, *Divine Economy: theology and the market*, London, Routledge, 2000, p. 270.

16. I want to express my gratitude to Aaron Riches for his reading of this work and his punctual suggestions.

II. The Bible and Bread

Stones into Bread: Why Not?
Eucharist – Koinonia – Diaconate

ÉRICO JOÃO HAMMES

Socio-cultural studies of early Christianity demonstrate the importance of table fellowship in Jesus' actions and those of the New Testament communities.[1] Bread and the Kingdom of God are associated one with another in Jesus' actions to the extent that we could call his table fellowship with sinners an 'acted parable' of divine concern for the poor, a strict parallel between table fellowship and the Kingdom of God. Three basic structures appear in this relationship: bread as temptation; bread as food and table fellowship; and the identification of Jesus as the bread of life. Starting from this statement, is it possible to work out a Christological – or even Christic – meaning of bread (food)? If so, what are the repercussions of its lack? And how do we interpret Jesus on the basis of hunger or meals?

I. Bread: a temptation?

The Synoptic gospels include an account of Jesus being tempted after his baptism (cf Mark 1.12–13; Matthew 4.1–11; Luke 4.1–13), and one of the temptations is to turn stones into loaves of bread (Matthew 4.3) or a stone into a loaf of bread (Luke 4.3). Leaving aside discussions of their historicity,[2] the stories as a whole form 'a unified literary composition, dominated by a theological reflection': Jesus' faithfulness to the Father, refusing to use his power to an end other than for which he was sent.[3]

The temptation to turn stones into loaves of bread evokes the Israelite recalling of a conflict with YHWH arising from the hunger and thirst they suffered in the desert: 'For you [Moses and Aaron] have brought us out into this wilderness to kill this whole assembly with hunger' (Exodus 16.3; cf Numbers 11; Psalms 78.19–21; 105.40); 'Why did you [Moses] bring us out of Egypt, to kill us and our children and livestock with thirst?' (Exodus 17.3; Numbers 20.4). While in itself appearing to be a contradiction of the Lord, suffering from hunger also reveals the vulnerability of God: instead of satisfying hunger, God is capable of suffering it. Satisfying hunger can be a simple act of power, since food brings with it the seduction of dominion and lordship. The power of bread represents the other face of the power of the sword. This is what the prophets are denouncing when they condemn exploitation through the sale of wheat (Amos 8.5; Hosea 12.8). Suffering hunger in solidarity, therefore, is the beginning of service.

This basic structure of temptation associated with bread can also be found in John's Gospel, when, after the multiplication of loaves and fishes, 'when Jesus realized that they were about to come and take him by force to make him king, he withdrew again to the mountain by himself'. (6.15) The starting point for a Christological reading of overcoming hunger lies, then, in understanding the ambiguity of the power of bread. The gospels show Jesus refusing not just to invoke the divine power on his own behalf but also to exercise the power of dominion, based on bread, over others.

II. Jesus' table fellowship

A second level of a Christological approach to hunger is provided by considering the importance of table fellowship in Jesus' life,[4] shown in his meals with publicans and sinners, in the 'multiplication of loaves', and in the communal nature of his everyday eating.

(a) Jesus regularly shares meals in common

In Jesus' life, as in the society of his time, gathering around a table formed the habitual way of establishing social bonds and roles, as well as establishing values and status.[5] In biblical Judaism, furthermore, it expresses a particular relationship to the Lord, the origin of gifts received. So, while the gospels do not dwell on descriptions of Jesus' daily table fellowship[6] ,they do mention the accusation, formulated by Matthew, of being 'a glutton and a drunkard, a friend of tax collectors and sinners' (11.19). In contrast with those of John the Baptist, Jesus' disciples 'cannot fast while the bridegroom is with them' (Mark 2.19 and par.). With the reservations due from a historical-critical viewpoint, there are frequent references to 'being together' at table. In Mark 14.18, immediately before the paschal supper but while they were already eating, Jesus addressed the twelve saying, 'One of you will betray me, one who is eating with me.' In John 12.1–2 he is described as dining in the house of Lazarus, whom he had raised from the dead. In the parallel texts of Matthew 26.6–13 and Mark 14.3–9, he is at the house of Simon the leper. In some passages that do not specifically mention a meal, the context and vocabulary identity one as the occasion. This is what seems to be happening at the house of Simon (Peter) in Mark 1.29–31 and parallels. After being healed, Simon's mother-in-law begins to serve (*diakonéo*) Jesus and the disciples. On his visit to Martha and Mary (see Luke 10.38–42), 'a woman named Martha welcomed him into her home' and is then described as 'distracted by her many tasks' (*diakonían*).

The discourse sending out the seventy-two disciples recommends that in the houses they go to, they 'eat and drink whatever they provide' (Luke 10.7). Despite the parallel texts being silent on this point (cf Luke 9.1–6; Matthew 10.1–16; Mark 3.13–19), Mark and Matthew do not contain the order, 'Take nothing for your journey, no staff, nor bag, nor bread' (Luke 9.3): going to townships, staying in the houses they go into, implies sharing at their tables.[8] Jesus, them took his meals in company, and surprised people by including publicans and sinners among that company.

In the early church, meals taken in common, strictly associated with the Eucharist and sometimes indistinguishable from it, are mentioned as part of the Christian way of life (cf Acts 2.42, 46; 27.35; 1 Corinthians 17.34). The roots of this practice should possibly be sought in Jesus himself, in the way he lived with the disciples.[9] Understood in this sense, meals form part of the *shalom* that should shine out from the community. The accounts of the appearance of the risen Christ, bathed in an atmosphere of peace, present meals as part of the experience of his presence. The peace and happiness that derive from the Kingdom of God find one of their most significant expressions in the shared table.

The messianic future is anticipated in meals and feasts.[10] The image of the eschatological feast (see Isaiah. 25.6) forms part of the Judaic tradition just as giving bread to the hungry embodies hope in the Lord (cf Psalms 133.15; 146.7), who takes of his own and gives them food in due season (Psalm 104.27f; cf 78.24). Nothing could be more normal, then, in the context of Jesus' preaching and actions, than to include satisfying hunger and celebrating a feast as part of the Kingdom of God. The happiness of the hungry is at hand, since they will be filled (cf Matthew 5.6; Luke 6.21). The Our Father (cf Luke 11.2–; Matthew 6.9–13), a communal prayer, perhaps to be said during meals, asks for the coming of the Kingdom and, as an integral part of this, the bread we need every day, forgiveness, and freedom from temptation. The definitive Kingdom will, therefore, be a great feast (cf Matthew 22.1–14; Luke 14.16–24) open to all who are willing to share at the table, with special invitations for those who do not normally have the chance.

In a word, Jesus' actions make a simple or a solemn meal a celebration of the presence of those invited, a re-integration of those who have been scattered and then return to the parental home (cf Luke 15.11–32), and an anticipation of the final Kingdom.

(b) Crowds invited to Jesus' table

The four gospels bear witness to the feeding of a great crowd that had gathered to hear Jesus: Mark 6.34–44, par. Matthew 14.14–21; Luke 9.11b–17; John 6.1–15; Mark 8.1–9, par. Matthew 15.32–8. Parts of these narratives are duplicated, but an original historical nucleus seems certain. Prominent among the principal elements present are the messianic formulation expressed in the numbers, the role of the disciples, indicating their serving function, and the way Jesus is concerned, has 'compassion', for the crowds, 'because they were like sheep without a shepherd' (Mark 6.34). In a 'deserted place' (though not a desert), Jesus ventures to give the crowd who had listened to his words something to eat before sending them home. He does not offer them stones to be turned into loaves, but loaves and fishes. As the father of the family does according to Jewish custom, Jesus takes the loaves to share them out. With his eyes raised to heaven, in the attitude of a wonder-worker, he blesses the loaves and fishes and, in the gesture associated with a celebratory feast, breaks them and hands them to the disciples to distribute.[11]

What is essential in the accounts of 'multiplication of loaves' is the fact that they are presented as 'gift' miracles (*Geschenkwunder*).[12] They describe Jesus' intervention, on his own initiative, beyond expectation but in a discreet fashion. It is he, mercy personified, who gives to the crowds. The divine Kingdom he has proclaimed becomes food, at the same time as it is signified by the 'breaking of bread'. Just as the father of a family breaks bread at meals in the home, Jesus likewise distributes, through the disciples (apostles), the food for the start of this new age, fulfilling the promise of Mary's and the psalmist's canticle: 'He has filled the hungry with good things, and sent the rich away empty' (Luke 1.53; cf Psalm 107.9).

(c) Publicans and sinners at table with Jesus

The aspect of Jesus' table fellowship, frequently mentioned in the gospels, of sharing meals with 'publicans and sinners', deserves attention. The accusation of being a friend to publicans and sinners (cf Matthew 11.19, par. Luke 7.34) is reinforced by the meal in the house of Levi (Mark 2.16 and par.) and of Zacchaeus (cf Luke 19.1–10). The main significance, going beyond moral considerations, is openness to everyone. Meals cannot be restricted to selected groups on moral grounds, still less on social ones.[13] This is also the lesson that Simon the Pharisee and his guests have to learn (cf Luke 7.36–50). Jesus came to save sinners, not the just; he came to heal the sick and not the healthy. The essence lies in the specific application of mercy.

Jesus' table fellowship or communion at table amounts to a celebration of the Kingdom of God and joy in its presence.[14] Despite not having anywhere to lay his head, Jesus breaks bread and boundaries to allow the Kingdom of hope and the future to break in for those who are hungry and have no shepherd. The accusation made against Jesus that he was 'a glutton and a drunkard' witnesses to the envy of those who could not endure his socializing with the *'am ha arez* (the people of the earth), the ordinary people.[15]

III. The Last Supper

Despite the historical uncertainties regarding the nature of the Last Supper, concerning whether it was a paschal meal or not,[16] it is certain that before his death Jesus celebrated a farewell meal, something intimately linked to both Judaic tradition and to his own death and resurrection. This meal represents the culmination of Jesus' practice of using meals as *diákonos* and moulds the group of disciples into a community based on human–divine table fellowship (*koinonía*) and service (*diakonía*), in fidelity to the Word and the Spirit. The accounts of 'multiplication of loaves' and the parable of the eschatological banquet in particular point in the same direction: Jesus is *hó diákonos*, the one who serves (at table) and who sets the table, open to all.

(a) The Supper and new relationships

The Last Supper is redolent both of the history and culture of the Jewish people and of the inauguration of a new era in Jesus. In this context, three aspects in particular stand out: the account in itself, as it appears in the Synoptics and in Paul (1 Corinthians 11.23–6), in the Johannine narrative, with the washing of feet (John 13), and, finally, the discourse on the bread of life (John 6). In the Pauline and Synoptic accounts, what stands out is the strict relationship with Jesus' final *pasch*, with actions and words pointing to

Jesus as the one indicated by the Passover, whose life put at risk will be the vehicle for a new beginning. The words spoken over the bread and cup translate this meaning of founding a new community (*koinonía*), a new covenant, which calls to mind death and resurrection – of Jesus himself, that is – through bread and wine. Just as the bread is broken to be distributed, so Jesus will likewise be broken and torn to pieces on the cross. This, however, will not be the last word. The last word comes earlier; he himself will continue to be present in bread and wine, his body and blood, for those who come together in his name, themselves becoming part of this inviting, serving, self-sacrificing community.[1]

In John's Gospel, lacking the words spoken over the bread and the cup, the Last Supper is understood in the light of the discourse on the bread of life and the washing of feet. In the first place, in the discourse on bread, Jesus clearly cannot be seen as belonging in the line of a divinity or of a magical and miracle-working messiah. The multiplication of loaves should be understood as a sign (6.26) and not simply as bread. Jesus brings a greater abundance than Moses, and this serves as a sign of his true messiahship. The true bread clearly does not just multiply but satisfies fully: 'I am the bread of life' (6.35, 48), 'the living bread that came down from heaven' (6.51). This bread, however, becomes present in all its conflictivity, as body and blood to be consumed so as to guarantee life. In other words, John seems to indicate a community of destiny between Jesus and those who accept him as 'living bread' with the future this implies, passing through surrender on the cross to oneness with the Father (cf 6.44, 56f), and life in the Spirit (cf 6.63).

The washing of feet, finally, shows the existential depth of the Servant. Washing people's feet, while still being a service, can be a gesture of hospitality, of affection, or of slavish obligation.[18] As it is described, its meaning and scope are stressed. Loving to the end (cf 13.1) is also serving to the end. Love, washing the feet of others, is a sign of acceptance of love received: 'For I have set you an example, that you also should do as I have done to you' (13.15).

(b) Supper, cross, and sacrifice

Table fellowship, eating at a common table, with the Lord is one of the forms sacrifices take in the Old Testament. Different periods show various embodiments of this, some of them forming part of Judaic liturgy. Besides the paschal supper, there are other forms of 'sacrifice of wellbeing' (cf Leviticus 19.5–6).[19] These are the sacrifices Paul is referring to when, in 1

Corinthians 10.14–22, speaking of sacred meals, he asks: 'The cup of bless-ing that we bless, is it not a sharing in the blood of Christ? The bread that we break, is it not a sharing in the body of Christ? Because there is one bread, we who are many are one body, for we all partake of the one bread. [. . .] Are not those who eat the sacrifices partners in the altar?' It is worth recalling sacri-fices of this kind as the most adequate for speaking of the Eucharist.

Considering the Eucharist as 'sacrifice of wellbeing' sheds light on its relationship with the cross as well as on its sacrificial significance. The Eucharistic altar is not a holocaust altar but one where the Divine Mystery and human reality come together. It is the meeting point between Jesus' cross-resurrection and his being a meal. The Supper interprets the cross and not the other way round. By taking up the bread and the memorial cup, Jesus takes on his passion and resurrection as the consequence of his faithfulness to the Father and his table fellowship. He spills, so to speak, his blood, his historical life, in an offering to the Father (cf. Deuteronomy 12.23), so as then to be consumed in his crucified glorification, as an expression of human unity with the Father and of the Father with us in the Spirit. In other words, Jesus' earthly life, closed on the cross, is not the fullness of the divine offer-ing, since this is prolonged and made specific in every human being through the Eucharistic table fellowship. Humanity, called together in assembly in the Spirit, must share in the table or the altar to fulfil and enter into its destiny and the divine mission of being life. While the Eucharist cannot be understood without the cross, neither can the cross be understood without the Eucharist. We can then say that not just the passion, death, and resur-rection of Jesus but the whole of life is present in the Eucharist.

Conclusion: Jesus, *hó diákonos*, who came to serve at table

From what we have seen so far, the concept of the *diákonos*, the one who serves at table, is a fundamental criterion for understanding both Jesus and Christian and human life. As it transcends the value of replenishing or sustaining physical-biological energies, the significance of food is open. It can represent the quest for self as well as the quest for and encounter with others. From the biblical-textual point of view, it possesses a further signifi-cance as encounter with transcendence, as blasphemy, or as idolatry. By relating the origin of evil with the act of violating the prohibition on eating the fruit of a particular tree, the Bible identifies a re-signification of eating: if it becomes an end in itself, it ceases to be human.

The account of Jesus' temptation shows the unity between bread and word. The Jewish tradition, according to which the *Torah* itself become bread, allied to blessing (*brk*), bears within itself the movement to make the divinity that exists in bread into Word. By bringing the Word together with bread, the latter acquires meaning, becomes humanized, since bread needs to have a meaning for human beings. Bread without meaning makes no sense, jut as words without bread are falsehood. The Word, the setting for being-in-community, gives meaning to the bread, just as bread makes the Word concrete. Outside communion (*koinonía*) with other people and with God, both bread and word lose their meaning.

Hence also the emptiness (*vanitas*) inherent in the temptation to turn stones into bread. Bread derived from power and as a simple satisfaction of hunger, without the Word or – worse – against the Word, is not true food. Willingness to hear and live the Word – as opposed to giving way to the temptation to turn stones into loaves at Satan's suggestion – brings the consequence for Jesus that 'angels came and waited on him (*diêkónoun*)' (cf Matthew 4.11; Mark 1.13). Once emptying or despoiling has taken place, then space is opened for the divine presence. As opposed to easy miracles that manipulate mystery, the divine presence in the midst of creation shows itself in Jesus as discretion (*quenóse*): he lives more by the Word of God than by his own power, witnessing to a hidden, not a spectacular, mystery. In place of stones, he brings loaves. These are multiplied on being shared among all. They do not represent, therefore, accumulation for its own sake, but depend on someone producing them so that they can be shared, however few they may be. The Christic, divine, and God-related aspect lies not in aggrandizement but in the gift of sharing, so that the table can be prepared. Sharing at Jesus' table means extending it for more people, making space for others to eat, finding fulfilment in setting the table for those who are hungry. The table extended in this way becomes a feast, a banquet at which humankind and divine mystery mingle in mutual fellowship.

By presenting Jesus as *ho diakonôn* (one who serves [at table]: Luke 22.27), or as the one who 'came not to be served (*diakonethênai*) but to serve (*diakonêsai*)' (Mark 10.45; Matthew 20.28), the gospels show the essential relationship between Jesus and serving at table. Right up to the apparition narratives of the risen Christ, sharing bread or the act of eating are used as confirmatory signs of the resurrection. John's gospel carries on the same idea in the phrase 'bread of life', when it makes a theological reading, in *midrash* form, of the multiplication of the loaves. In the act of washing feet it places the same emphasis on serving as does the giving of body and blood in the Synoptics' accounts of the bread and cup at the Last Supper. Jesus of

Nazareth should be understood as the divine bending over deprived and needy humanity so as to restore it in its vitality. Confessing the Son in this way implies taking on the *diakonía* of human beings.

Feeding the hungry is, then, the praxic form of confessing the Master-Servant. 'When did we [. . .] not take care (*diêkonêsamen*) of you?', ask those rejected in the account of the last judgment (Matthew 25.44). Living for others, for the sake of their lives, and regarding the lives of other people as the content of our own existence, is the evidence of faith in the one who came to serve at table and not to be served. Recalling Andre Rublev's famous icon of the Trinity, we can say that the divine three-in-one are adored in the table service of the pilgrims who travel to the shanty towns, streets, refugee camps and hovels of present-day society.

In the light of the foregoing, I should like finally to suggest that the hunger for meaning, so often emphasized today, goes with the meaning of table fellowship. Accepting the face of the hungry as one's own other face is the beginning of coming to terms with oneself. As a result, personal and social maturity, as well maturity in faith, imply the ability to serve people at table, to make the hunger of others one's own, to set a table for many and, in the final analysis, for divine mystery, for the Absolute. The Eucharist becomes the beginning and the culmination of dinner tables, of politics, of science, of religions, and of national and international economies. The table set for the human race is, more than a matter of technology, a question of the meaning of human existence.

Translated by Paul Burns

Notes

1. For an overview of the main studies in English, see Jerome H. Neyrey, 'Reader's Guide to Meals, Food and Table Fellowship in the New Testament', at www.nd.edu/~jneyrey1/meals.
2. Cf J. Gnilka, *Das Matthäusevangelium*, Freiburg 1988, vol. 1, p. 83. The same author, in *ibid.*, p. 92, recalls J. Dupont as having defended the historicity of the temptation narratives (*Die Versuchungen Jesu in der Wüste*, Stuttgart 1969).
3. Cf J. Fitzmyer, The Gospel According to Luke (I-IX), New York 1981, pp. 508-9.
4. A good synthesis, from the point of view of inclusion, can be found in S. Yao, 'The Table Fellowship of Jesus with the Marginalized', *Journal of Asian Mission* 3 (2001), pp. 25-41, with a good bibliography; see also J. Becker, *Jesus von Nazareth*, Berlin & New York 1996, pp. 194-211.

5. Cf B. Janowski, 'Opfermahl', in G. Manfred and B. Lang, *Neues Bibel-Lexikon*, Düsseldorf & Zurich 2001, vol. 2, p. 43; M. E, Moore, 'Table Fellowship in the Gospels', at www.occ.edu/markmoore/meals (25 Jan. 2005).

6. E. Lohmeyer ('Vom urchristlichen Abendmahl' in *Theologische Rundschau*, Neue Folgen 9 (1937), pp. 168–227; 273–312) is quoted as the first modern author to draw attention to Jesus' table community: see R. Schwager, *Jesus I, Heilsdrama*, Innsbruck & Vienna 1990, pp. 192–6; also N. Perrin, *Rediscovering the Teaching of Jesus*, London 1967 (German ed. pp. 126–33); E. Schillebeeckx, *Jesus, an Experiment in Christology*, London & New York 1979 (Eng. trans. of *Jezus, het verhaal van en levende*, Bloemendal 1974: here German ed., pp. 177–203).

7. Schillebeeckx, *op. cit.*, p. 178.

8. J. D. Crossan, *The Historical Jesus: The Life of a Mediterranean Peasant*, New York 1993 (here German trans. 1994, pp. 439–461).

9. This is the opinion of N. Perrin, *op.cit.*, pp. 128–30.

10. On this see Becker, *Jesus von Nazareth*, pp. 194–211.

11. Cf R. Pesch, *Il vangelo di Marco*, Brescia 1982, p. 549.

12. This is how G. Theissen proposes to classify the multiplication of loaves, the miraculous catch (Luke 5.1–11) and the changing of water into wine: see 'Der historische Jesus' in *Der historische Jesus: ein Lehrbuch*, Göttingen 1996, p. 267.

13. On this characteristic see L. C. Susin, 'Eucaristia, pão de inclusão', *Tele-communicacão* 33 (2003), pp. 665–61. See also S. Yao, 'The Table Fellowship of Jesus', *art.cit.*

14. An aspect brought out especially by J. Sobrino in *Jesus the Liberator*, Tunbridge Wells & Maryknoll, NY, 1994, pp. 102–4 (Eng. trans. of *Jesucristo liberador. Lectura histórica-teológica de Jesús de Nazaret*, Madrid 1991).

15. Cf J. Gnilka, *Jesus von Nazaret. Botschaft und Geschichte*, Freiburg 1990, pp. 110–2.

16. The historical question relates to the differences in the chronological indicators between the Synoptics and John. In both, Jesus is crucified on the sixth day of the week, but while the Synoptics make this also the 15th of the month of Nisan and so the Jewish Passover, John speaks of the preparation day: 'Now it was the day of Preparation for the Passover' (John 19.14; cf 19.31), so the 14th day of Nisan.

17. 'The tradition of the supper [. . . in Mark] concludes the meals Jesus took with sinners (2.15ff) and the crowd (6.35ff; 8.1ff) and takes the disciples together into the passion': Gnilka, *Das Evangelium nach Markus*, 2, Zurich, Einsiedeln, Cologne 1979, p. 249.

18. Cf J. Konings, *Evangelho Segundo João*, Petrópolis 2000, p. 294. This is a humble service, 'but it as not just for slaves, but formed part of a wife's duties to her husband, and children's to their parents' (cf R. Schnackenburg, *Das*

Johannesevangelium, 5th ed. Freiburg 1986, vol. 3, p. 19 (Eng. trans. *The Gospel According to St John*, 3 vols., New York, 1968–82).

19. R. de Vaux distinguishes six forms of sacrifice in the Judaic tradition: holocaust, communion sacrifice, expiatory sacrifice, vegetable offerings, loaves of obligation, loaves of proposition, and offerings of incense. Note that several of these required sharing at table: see *Ancient Israel: Its Life and Institutions* (here Port. trans., pp. 453–61).

Nourishment in the Midst of Violence: The Biblical Stories about Elijah

MARIE-THERES WACKER

In no other narrative tradition in the Hebrew Bible the motive of food and drink occurs as frequently as it does in the stories around the prophet Elijah and his successor Elisha.[1] In what follows I will focus on the Elijah cycle 1 Kings 17 – 2 Kings 2 in order to explore the multi-layered meanings of the motive of food and feeding. My hermeneutical approach to the text is informed by historical and narrative analysis and looks for inner-biblical intertextuality.[2]

Elijah – the Word of God in world of violence

Like a flash of lightening, without any introduction, the character of Elijah appears on the textual stage. He passes on a word of God and thus he identifies himself as a prophet. He hurls it towards the ruler of the Northern kingdom Ahab: no rain shall fall during these years, as the God of Israel lives. Against the background of the preceding verses about the beginning of Ahab's rule this is a declaration of war: Ahab has built an altar for Baal (16.32), has offered him cultic reverence (16.31) and has thus recognized the authority of this god. This however the God of Israel will not tolerate. He sends his prophet to announce the non-appearance of rain. Thus images of lack of water, of drought and subsequent famine are evoked. It is now in the hands of Ahab, the king, to influence the fate of his country. Water and grain, the life and death of his kingdom will depend on his religious and political actions.

The character of Elijah is from the first to the last scene of the cycle cast in a narrative context of violence, related both to internal politics and religion and to external politics and war. This violence is initiated by those in power. However, Elijah himself is also implicated in it through his own actions. This seems to tie in with the framework of his appearance: as suddenly and 'thunder-like' as his first appearance is his final one. His 'ascension' in the chariot of fire (2 Kings 2.1–18) can be read as the delivery of the prophet; yet he leaves behind a world in which suffering and injustice continue to dominate. It is therefore all the more remarkable that a number of contradicting aspects are connected especially with the motive of food and this image.

Food –nourishment and sign of the presence of God

The first small narrative unit (17.2–6) leads us to a brook full of water on the other side of the Jordan and thus far away from the royal palace. This is where Elijah is asked to go following a word of God, there he shall drink – and also eat, as ravens feed him by divine command with bread and meat. Elijah will not have to suffer from the drought which human beings and animals might have begun to suffer elsewhere in the country. Closeness to animals, such as Elijah experiences it now, is perhaps a particular characteristic of prophets.[3] This scene also has something miraculous: Elijah has his food handed down from heaven, like once upon a time Israel received manna and quails in the desert (Exodus 16.8–35). For the first time in the Elijah narratives we encounter a special kind of food which is not only nourishment in the most elementary way, but which also points beyond that to the close relationship between Elijah and his God.

Food – nourishment and sign of abundance

The second small narrative unit (17.7–16) begins with a reference to the increasing lack of water. Elijah is now led well out of Ahab's country, to Zarephath, into Phoenician territory. At the heart of this unit is the life-threatening suffering of a widow. The woman has enough flour and water left to prepare one last cake for herself and her son before they face death from starvation. Elijah challenges her nevertheless to share the last she has with him, and she agrees to do so. And then another miracle happens: all three have enough to eat.

The opening of the narrative likens the widow to the ravens: like them she is an instrument sent by God to provide for the prophet. But such instrumentalization is by no means all: it is central to the narrative that the woman does not ignore the stranger at the city gate but that she, in spire of her own extreme suffering, welcomes him as a guest. The Phoencian woman treats Elijah in the way prescribed by the laws of the God of Israel. She, the non-

Israelite, fulfils the Torah of Israel, while the king of Israel walks all over God's commandments. It is therefore possible that she, the Phoenician woman in the land of Baal is able to experience the power of the God of Israel. Here too food is both basic sustenance and it also – by its sheer abundance – points to the presence of God.

The third narrative unit (17.17–24) adds to the life-threatening lack of food a further threat: the death of the son, the only one who would look after the widow when she herself is no longer able to do so. Again the God of Israel shows his power through the prophet so that the widow now declares her allegiance to this God.

Food – nourishment and sign of resistance

The new opening in chapter 18.1 reconnects Elijah with Ahab. The prophet is now supposed to tell the king that the time without rain will come to an end. Prior to their actual encounter, two scenes illustrate the situation in the country and at court (18.2–6.7–16). The king himself and Obadiah, the man in charge of the palace, go out in search of sources of water where there might be some bits of grass still growing so that at least the cattle could be saved. Now, in the third year of drought, the suffering has reached its threatening climax which begins to have an impact on the lives of the animals.

But we also hear about another kind of threat to the lives of the people, religious persecution emerging from the royal palace. In this situation the man in charge of the palace intervenes and provides fifty prophets of JHWH, whom he managed to save from being assassinated by the king's order, with food and drink (see 18.4,13). In doing so Obadiah (whose name means 'servant of JHWH') has set himself on the side of the God of Israel and saved human lives. The food which he provides sustains lives and is also a symbol of (religious and) political resistance.

Two women who provide nourishment

Behind the religious persecution against the cult of JHWH is Jezebel, the royal consort from Phoenicia. In the Elijah and Elisha narratives she is cast as a powerful and also incredibly evil character. She is the prototype of the 'strange woman' who leads the Israelite astray to the path of godlessness[4]: Her marriage to Ahab follows Ahab's worship of Baal (1 Kings 16.31). She persecutes the prophets of JHWH (18.4,13) and at the same time protects large numbers of the prophets of Baal and Asherah whom she feeds at the royal table (18.19). Thus she is cast as the counterpoise to the other 'strange woman' in the Elijah narratives, the Phoenician widow from Zarephath, who herself provides food for a prophet.[5] On both sides there is a woman who provides food – for one this leads to life for herself, her son and the prophet who is her guest; for the other it will lead to a violent death, that of her prophetic followers (1 Kings 18.40) and eventually her own (see 2 Kings 9.30–37).

Meat and water as signs of the manifestation of divine power

The first encounter between the prophet and the king since the end of the rain is once again characterized by confrontation (see 18.17–19). Ahab accuses Elijah of having brought suffering over Israel, and this may refer to the drought who Elijah had foretold (see 17.1). The king therefore connects the problem with the powerful word of the prophet which has literally brought about the disaster. Elijah however throws the accusation back at the king and elevates it to the level of religious politics which, looking at the dynamics of the narrative, is what determines the events in the first place. There will be no rain until the question 'Baal or JHWH' is resolved.

This time the king's people are involved too. Indeed, their role is also a crucial one: they are challenged by Elijah to make their decision and in the end burst out their acclamation: 'JHWH is the God!' In doing so they put themselves on the side of Elijah whose name means: 'My God is JHWH'. At the height of suffering the tide-turning actions of the monarch are no longer sufficient. All the people in Israel have to decide for themselves and in doing so, in an almost democratic manner, share in determining the direction of religious politics.[6]

The decision takes place on 'Mount Carmel' (see 18.20–40). In this context there is no need to discuss if this is indeed a historic holy place. If the narrative chooses a mountain as the location for the decision, this is most certainly because one can imagine that Baal, but also JHWH, would choose a mountain as the preferred place for an epiphany and therefore as suitable for the sacrifice and test described here.

For both gods a ram is prepared as a sacrifice – there is no more talk about the lack of water for the animals; rather there is even enough water to fill the moat which has been dug around the sacrifice. The narrative tracks life the scene on Mount Carmel out of their context as a special time and special space; in every sense of the word this is an exceptional situation.[7] In particular the meat and the water do not serve as food for anyone, but both become objects which are used for the power of the stronger God to manifest itself in the fire which falls from heaven and consumes both.

Nourishment as anticipation of the end of suffering

The final scene in chapter 18 (18.41–46) tells the story of the arrival of the rain. Elijah asks Ahab to eat and to drink for the sound of the rain could already be heard. The king is asked to do precisely what for many around him is no longer possible because of the famine, and he is now asked to anticipate the coming restoration of the balance. The king's eating and drinking become signs of the end of the disaster and anticipation of the forthcoming time when there will once again be food for all.

Nourishment from heaven for new life

Exegetes have described chapters 17 and 18 as the 'drought composition'. In it the motive of rain failing to appear and then appearing once again is skilfully connected with chapter 19, not least in connected with the food motive which will no longer play a role in the remaining chapters of the Elijah cycle.

After the final scene in chapter 18 the drought may well be over. However, the religious persecution, instigated at the court in Samaria and tied in narrative terms to the character of Jezebel, is by no means over. While she has got the murder of JHWH's prophets on her conscience, Elijah has ordered the slaughter of Baal's prophets to which Jezebel in turn responds with her own threat to murder Elijah. Once again the prophet has to flee from the court (19.1–2).

Elijah escapes to the southern part of Judah, far away from the sphere of the influence of Ahab and Jezebel. On a first level the description in chapter 19.3–8 matches the state of Elijah's soul. He longs for death, separates from his companions and goes to a part of the country which is empty and deserted by human beings. There he lies down as if to anticipate his death in his sleep. In this situation however he receives strength which comes from a messenger sent by God. Elijah receives water in a pitcher (the Hebrew word used for it reminds of the jug of oil used by the Phoenician widow), and a loaf of bread like the one prepared for him by the widow (19.6; see 17.12–14). Through these textual references God's messenger is given a human face, but also the light of being God's messenger is in turn cast back on the widow.

For Elijah receiving once again food and strength in a miraculous way means new courage to live, so that he is able to continue to travel on his remaining journey.

On a second level we can discover in the descriptions in this scene elements of a rite of passage, through which the destination of the journey, God's mountain, is moved into focus. First of all, Elijah leaves his servant behind (19.3) and is therefore left to his own devices. Then he goes into the desert, far away from human habitation, to a place where only very few plants will grow, and there he lies down to sleep (19.5). In his sleep he hears the voice of God's messenger and receives strength through food and drink. This sleep also takes on the meaning of a healing event and the crossing over a threshold to the place which now becomes the destination of Elijah's way through the desert. And in turn: only through food from heaven which he receives twice on this threshold Elijah becomes able to go on his journey to meet God.

Farewell meal – disruption – miraculous feeding

The narrative of God's appearance on the Holy Mountain (19.9–18) can certainly be understood, as has been frequently done by Old Testament scholars, as a thwarting of all too fixed ideas as to how the God of Israel makes himself known; not in a whirlwind, not in an earthquake (!), not in a fire, but, to use Martin Buber's paradoxical expression in a 'voice of silence soaring away'. Great care is taken to make JHWH audible but by no means visible. In doing so the scene is also reminiscent of God appearing to Moses, likewise in a cave on the Holy Mountain (Exodus 33.18–23). Thus the scene takes on dimensions way beyond the immediate context of the Elijah cycle. Elijah is cast as a prophet like Moses (see Deuteronomy 18.18). In addition, they also raise fundamental questions as to how one could speak about God in an appropriate manner. Within the context of the Elijah cycle the epiphany of JHWH is connected with a commission that goes much further: by anointing kings the prophet is meant to get involved in national politics and at the same time to provide a successor who will continue his calling as a prophet.

How this calling is implemented is told in the last scene in chapter 19 (19.19–21). Elisha is in the middle of ploughing a field when Elijah confronts him with the challenge to follow him by throwing his cloak over him. Elisha's immediate reaction is what initially looks like rather strange feeding: he slaughters the oxen which was ploughing, uses the ploughing equipment to prepare them for cooking and feeds them to 'the people' (19.21). In the context of the narrative this abundant feeding takes on the characteristics of a farewell meal with which Elisha dismisses the people who worked for him, and perhaps in addition to that the complete rescinding of his life up to that point, the destruction of those material things which he had hitherto used to feed himself and his family. Looking forward to the Elisha narratives we seem see once again the dimension of a miraculous feeding: a small scene in 2 Kings 4.42–44 tells the story how Elisha provides food for 'the people (this is now the group of people among whom he lives) – this time he uses what little there is, and yet all are fed.

Elisha: nourishment against want

In the Elisha cycle too the motive of food remains central and embedded in the themes of life and death. Here too it is concentrated in the first part of the cycle (2 Kings 2.19–8.15), chapters 4, 6 and 7 to be precise. The religious and political conflict which had been so important for the Elijah narratives is of hardly any significance for these narratives; it will come to the fore once again in 2 Kings 9. In the Elisha narratives, focused on the food motive, other kinds of conflicts come to light; they are far more concrete and far less laden with symbolism.[8]

There are no analogies to the narratives in 2 Kings 6–7 in the Elijah cycle. In a situation full of tension due to external politics, Elisha suggests to the king that a group of Aramaic spies which have been tracked down should not be killed but lavished with royal hospitality. In a non-violent but highly ironic way it would be made clear to them that they stood no chance what-soever against Israel's counter intelligence (6.1–23). Within the narrative framework of war, occupation and severe famine we are then led to look at two women who in their utter despair had killed and eaten the child of one of them. This situation of utter misery is then seen as a result of the king's failure. Elisha sets against it the image of hope for abundant feeding which will soon be realised in the miraculous rescinding of the occupation (6.24–7.20).

In the narratives in 2 Kings 4 we encounter a number of motives with which we are already familiar from our reading of the Elijah narratives. Elisha too encounters a widow in her want (2 Kings 4.1–7). The scene about the miraculous flow of oil, which she is then able to sell in order to protect her sons from being sold into slavery, does not have the ambiguity of its parallel in the Elijah cycle (1 Kings 17.7–14). Instead it is aimed directly and in a much more concrete way at the woman's socio-political suffering and its alleviation through the help of God and the prophet. The story of the woman of Shunem who feeds the man of God and whose son is brought back to life by Elisha (2 Kings 4.8–37) is reminiscent of the respective narrative in the Elisha cycle in 1 Kings 17. In the Elisha cycle however the interaction between the woman and the man of God is much more central. In addition, there is a strong emphasis on the miraculous power of the prophet who has life and death at his disposal (and thus it also contains some disturbing aspects; see only 2 Kings 2.23–25). This aspect seems to determine the further narratives which revolve around the motive of food: in a time of famine Elisha miraculously provides food for the community of prophets in which he lives (2 Kings 4.42–44) and saves it from poisoned food (4.38–41). This community is cast as one which fights social injustice and material want; this it takes on characteristics of the counter-cultural.

Jesus in the tracks of Elisha

In the gospel stories about Jesus miraculously feeding those who had followed him, there are obvious reminiscences of Elisha's multiplication of food.[9] In this tradition the Jesus stories share some real utopia: at least already in the small circle of those who follow the prophet, no-one will suffer hunger because one shares the necessities of life. Yet, even more so, even the Elisha narrative contains the little aside 'they ate and had some left' (2 Kings 4.42). This forecasts the abundance which will turn the miraculous feeding narratives of the New Testament into Eucharistic stories, the gratitude with which the earliest believers in Christ remembered their meal fellowship in which they celebrated the promise of God's reign. As the gospels remember Elijah – alongside his significance as a prophet of the end times[10] and as a representative of prophecy in general[11] – with regard to his power over sickness and death[12], the first believers in Christ obviously found in Elijah the point of contact in his prophetic table fellowship where life became possible against a world of violence.

Translated by Natalie K. Watson

Further reading

Robert L. Cohn, 'The Literary Logic of 1 Kings 17–19' *JBL* 101 (1982), pp. 333–350.

Frank Crüsemann, *Elia – die Entdeckung der Einheit Gottes. Eine Lektüre der Erzählungen über Elia und seine Zeit*, Gütersloh, Kaiser, 1997.

Kyung Sook Lee, 'Die Königs-Bücher. Frauen-Bilder ohne Frauen-Wirklichkeit' in *Kompendium feministische Bibelauslegung* edited by Luise Schottroff and Marie-Theres Wacker, Gütersloh, 1998, pp. 130–145 (an American translation is in preparation).

Ursula Vock, 'Versorgung und Lebenslust. Predigt über 1. Könige 17,8–16' in: *Weiberwirtschaft. Frauen – Ökonomie – Ethik* edited by Heidi Berhard Filli et al., Luzern, 1994, pp. 121–138.

Jürgen Werlitz, *Die Bücher der Könige* Neuer Stuttgarter Kommentar AT 8, Stuttgart 2002.

Notes

1. The so-called Elijah cycle in 1 Kings 17.1 – 2 Kings 2.18 is interwoven with the narrative about the Northern king Ahab and queen Jezebel. These begin in 1 Kings 16.29 and stretch to 1 Kings 22.40 (end of Ahab) and 2 Kings 9.37 (end of Jezebel). The character Elijah first appears in 1 Kings 19.16,19–21. The cycle of Elisha stories begins with 2 Kings 2.1–18, at once the end of the Elijah cycle, and stretches to 2 Kings 8.15. In 2 Kings 8.16 a new block of narratives begins. In it Elisha only appears once (9.1f). This however is the starting point for the subsequent events of the so-called Jehu revolution. The narrative ends with 2 Kings 13.14–21 and 22–25, the death of Elisha and the end of Hazael who with Elisha's help had become king of Aram (see 2 Kings 8.7–15 and already 1 Kings 19.15).

2. I take it as a prerequisite that the Elijah narrative in its present context is the result of a multi-phase history of development and will not undertake any further historical-critical analysis of this here.

3. See the female donkey of Balaam who seeks to protect him from the wrath of God (Numbers 22.22–35), and see also Mark 1.13 (Jesus and the wild beasts).

4. See for this stereotype also 1 Kings 11.1–8 (the many strange woman who lead Solomon astray to worshipping idols) and especially Proverbs 5–7.

5. On the one hand this illustrates that the Deuternoministic theology, which is the origin of this contrast, does not defame all non-Israelite women by default. On the other hand Lee Kyung-Sook points out that this theology obviously does have a problem with women in power and with powerful women and therefore denounces such women in its narratives (see Jezebel as well as Athalijah 2 Kings 11 and Maacha 1 Kings 15.9–13).

6. This element of the narrative, the nation as a whole deciding, may lead us to

conclude that there may have been an independent source for the story of the 'divine judgement on Mount Carmel', but in the characteristic style of this particular text it can be read as I have suggested here.

7. This is how the scene can be understood in its context without having to dispute that it might possibly contain an older tradition which might have existed independently from its present context.

8. From a historical-critical perspective, the Elijah narratives are regarded as earlier and more original, while the related Elisha narratives are later imitations.

9. See Matthew 14.13–21 and 15.32–38 and parallels and 2 Kings 4.42–44.

10. See the frequent references in the gospels to the question of the return of Elijah.

11. See the story of the Transfiguration in Mark 9.2–8 and parallels.

12. See the direct reference of Luke 4.25–26 to 1 Kings 17.6ff, but also Luke 7.11–17 to 1 Kings 17.17–24 and 2 Kings 4.32–37.

From the Depths of Hunger

ANNE FORTIN

Introduction

Mark's Gospel links Jesus' last meal to his statement that Judas will betray him. From the action of the one who will 'deliver' him to the 'take; this is my body', two 'eucharistic' understandings are introduced. I propose to approach the institution of the Eucharist by taking these two ways of understanding reality as an illustration, an illustration that will be based on Augustine's definition of 'sign', the foundation of our whole understanding of the sacraments. To do this, I shall first expound the central element of the meal, bread, in a re-reading of some passages of Mark, which will open the way to a reflection on the meaning of the Eucharist considered as a narrative.

I. The figure of bread (Mark 6.30–44; 8.1–9)

The figure of bread immediately evokes the two multiplications of loaves in Mark's gospel. In chapter 6 Jesus, seeing the great crowd, 'had compassion for them, because they were like sheep without a shepherd; and he began to teach them many things'. The disciples wanted to send the crowd away so that they could go and buy something to eat, but Jesus takes a different approach to the crowd's hunger. 'You give them something to eat': he gives the disciples back their capacity to give. Hunger cannot be reduced to an empty space to fill; it rather leads us into the relationship of giving. Jesus thereby places the disciples in their role as shepherds to the sheep who are waiting for a narrative, which cannot be reduced to the satisfaction of a need. This pastoral attitude points up the different reactions of Jesus and the disciples: the dynamic of giving on one side; resignation, powerlessness, and failure to take responsibility on the other. Now that the disciples have been 'recognized' by the crowd as shepherds alongside Jesus, he re-establishes them in the specificity of the position of a shepherd in relation to his sheep, in the situation of giving. This is gratuitousness, totally opposed to exchange, the mercantile aspect.

Another element is added to this logic of giving: the opening-up of space made possible by Jesus' verbal decision: 'He looked up to heaven, and blessed and broke the loaves, and gave them to his disciples.' The horizontal line is drawn out, and the vertical is opened up: the dynamic of giving situates the objects given here in a quite other space, which brings in a third party, which enables the gifts to be distributed. And so reality is transformed, and the relationship with the space that rules connections is shifted, which is the 'miracle' properly so called.

The space opened up by hunger thus produces two processes: that of exchange and that of gift. One process is binary, mercantile; the other is ternary, in which Trinitarian space in its circulatory dimension makes its appearance.[1] The space opened reveals the nature of the link between the subjects (sheep-shepherd): how the lack signalled by hunger is received and understood, what faith is thereby engaged. What then becomes apparent is that things on their own – the accumulation of things – cannot satisfy hunger, and that the Trinitarian dynamic creates a new relationship to hunger, as to all suffering, to everything that concerns human nature, by taking the weight of humanity away from it. Jesus does not separate the two actions – the giving of his word and the gift of his body – but addresses the same space of suffering, physical and spiritual, in both. And the disciples understand nothing of all this, since their hearts are hardened.

The second 'multiplication of loaves', in chapter 8, poses the problem of this hunger more radically: 'If I send them away hungry to their homes, they will faint on the way.' There follows the same sequence of events: Jesus gives thanks, breaks the loaves, and hands them to his disciples for them to distribute to the crowd. He thereby teaches the disciples the process of giving by making them givers in the logic of a word open to the third party. This is how the word becomes flesh; this is how Jesus brings a new reality about by the gift of his word, of which bread becomes a figure. This is how 'nothing will be impossible with God' (Luke 1.37).

This characterization of the figure of bread enables us to put a different meaning on it in the account of the institution, where it is then attached to the figure of wine. This figure, as dramatic as it is in itself, then points to the parable of the murderous winegrowers, which requires a detour before coming to the Last Supper itself.

II. The parable of the murderous winegrowers

This parable (Mark 12.1–12) introduces the fruit of the vine. In this parable the fruit of the vine becomes a factor of the isolated power of giving: it is not even inserted into a process of exchange, since it is seized, appropriated, outside any relationship, even a mercantile one. It is the end point of reference to objects, where people are ready to kill anyone who interferes with the possession of an object. The fruit becomes an inheritance with no affiliation, no link, no commitment. The object is wrapped in greed, with its value no longer related to anything outside itself. Cupidity thereby deprives the object of any interaction, of any life. The inheritance retains nothing but the death of its original significance, this death being brought about by taking the fruit immediately. The parable describes how human beings drink the 'fruit of the vine' in the time-space of the murder, reducing it to a blood spilt for death. Not again drinking the fruit of the vine 'until that day when I drink it new in the kingdom of God' (Mark 14.25) therefore consists in removing it from the relationship of objectivization in which human beings have enclosed it, in order to reinsert it in the space of the filial link, the kingdom of God, and the time of the novelty of a covenant made for the sake of human beings, not against them. The seizing of the inheritance, the vine, by the wicked tenants suspends the enjoyment of this fruit by the true heirs: it will be drunk in the kingdom of God – another time, another space.

But what link can we establish between the figure of bread, as interpreted here, and the figure of wine, fruit of the vine? And above all, how are these figures related to the Last Supper? We need to look more closely at Jesus' actions to understand these links.

III. The Last Supper

The Last Supper has nothing to say about hunger, nor about an inheritance, since it is the ritual of the Covenant. The space into which it opens is not explicitly that of hunger but that of need for salvation, reiterated, reinscribed in temporality through the means of a ritual meal. This however clearly evokes a space analogous to that of hunger by opening up a space of clamour for salvation. How does bread fit into this space? And how does wine fit in as inheritance, as prefiguring of the kingdom of God? How will it allow us to identify and name the heirs to the kingdom?

While the 'loaves affairs' left space for the process of giving among people, the Last Supper sets the gift of bread in the context of the covenant. It will no longer be just the bread of life, sown and harvested, that is given, but it will be a bread bearing the weight of death and of a body given for life. How can the play of life and death have come to be radicalized to such an extent in the figure of bread? It is because between the loaves of the 'multiplications' and the bread of the Last Supper there comes the parable of the murderous winegrowers, in which the fruit of the vine becomes charged with hatred, murder, and spilt blood. And while the disciples had understood nothing about the 'loaves affairs', by a sad paradox the scribes and the elders had understood that 'he had told this parable against them' (Mark 12.12). What is brought together at the Last Supper is openness to salvation through the conjoining of bread, word, body given and blood shed. The Last Supper conjugates the euphoria of the gift of bread and life against the background of blood shed, the result of imposture and seizure. The new covenant carries all these dimensions to the heart of the opened space of hunger, where human beings always count on their cries to God being heard.

IV. The bread-sign

The bread given in this way cannot be reduced to an object, for what the biblical texts show us is that this bread does not exist outside the gesture of the gift taken by human words to God. This bread cannot even find a place in the market economy alone, since this implies impossibility for human beings on their own, as the consternation of the disciples shows. Yet nothing is impossible for God: by inscribing its word in the word given to human beings by God, the word of thanksgiving, which turns and offers itself to God, transforms reality by inscribing the word among human beings and thereby transforms bread into the presence of this word.

Going back to the biblical text in this way allows us to take a fresh look at Augustine's traditional definition of sign applied to the Eucharist: 'A sign is something that at one and the same time presents itself to the senses and presents something other than itself to the spirit.'[2] The whole of tradition revolves around this definition, which I take here in the sense of theory of sign rather than according to its varying interpretations throughout history.

In effect, Augustine is proposing a theory of sign that links what 'presents itself' to the one who receives it: the two wings of the definition imply that the relationship to significance, to understanding, cannot immediately be decoded, since this relationship implies its passage to the subject who receives it. 'The spirit', according to Augustine, is the consciousness of an interpreter subject comprising the arrival point of *what 'presents itself'*. In this way, the subject has a part to play, since between the 'fact of bread' and the process of giving inscribed in it a space is created in which a word is to be heard, where the subject has to be 'hungry', meaning being in a state of suspense, in need of salvation in order to hear what is being addressed to him by this sign. 'The spirit', that part of human nature that cannot be reduced to 'facts', will integrate this *something other* than *what 'presents itself'* into its act of reception. The texts narrating the multiplication of loaves indicate that it is then a matter of liberating the sign of bread from its enclosure in 'the objective order of value'. According to Augustine's definition, the sign cannot be detached from its relationship to the one who produces it or to the one who receives it. Consequently, it exists 'in the order of arbitrariness and non-value, regulated by pact'[3], which does not weaken it, as the positivist thinking of recent centuries might suppose, but, on the contrary, makes it a sign 'for the life' of human beings.

This double dimension of sign, being at once signifier and link to the interpreter subject, says in other words what the biblical text stated of the Eucharistic sign as to what is signified – bread, word, body – and as to the link between subjects, from gift to reception. The role of gift proper to the shepherd therefore deserves to be stressed as against the possible outcome that would separate the sign as object from the subjects: 'You give them something to eat' leads the disciples to commit themselves to the giving process, to become responsible for the gift. This part of the action, also stressed in the Last Supper text by the two mentions of 'take', stands in contrast to Judas, who reaches out his hand and takes, before there has been a word of giving – in reference to the seizure by the murderous winegrowers. Here there is no more than seizing, appropriating the bread and the body of Jesus to hand it over, which in fact destroys what is signified itself – and the inheritance with it: is Judas laying his hand on the Body of Christ or the body of Jesus? Will what he gets from it be a sign of life or of death? Does the bread he has taken for himself still have value as shared gift, or is it just one piece of merchandise exchanged for another? It becomes clear that Judas' act of seizing has not succeeded in taking the Body of Christ, which is always present in the community that calls to mind his death and resurrection. In the biblical text, the drama of the Last Supper is played out again at Jesus' arrest: 'while [Jesus] was still speaking, Judas [. . .] arrived; and with him there was a crowd with swords and clubs' (Mark 14.43). The word is interrupted, and the body is reduced to an object, but the Word will live on, in a different way and in another place, in speaking subjects.

So the sign is to be received and interpreted in the listening it produces, in the memory it awakens. Between the significance and the subject who receives it a space is formed, that of a spoken word which is given out but still has to be understood by and to reverberate among those who hear it. The word spoken has to become incarnate, this word has to become flesh in each of those who hear it.[4]

It is thus that the bread bears the memory of the movement of the word of thanksgiving toward the Father. The sign consequently takes the bread out of the register of objects and allows a link to be formed between what 'presents itself' and the word spoken and called to mind, summoning the subject in whom the word becomes flesh to listen.

Augustine's traditional definition gives an account of a process of linkage among the different aspects just evoked. So, the subject is called to interpret the sign of bread so as to take it out of a mercantile process and also out of a purely sacrificial logic. The sign of bread can be understood only on the basis of the words that have been spoken of it, considered both from the angle of what they say and from that of the action of giving. This is where the subject of faith's memory of the words spoken comes in: memory is a route that re-establishes the relationship of the sign to the word spoken ('Remember how he told you . . .' [Luke 24.6]). But this route can be trodden only by subjects summoned by this word: memory is not an abstract mechanism that functions on its own outside the subject. So, just as bread is not a simple 'symbol' to be decoded automatically on the basis of a pre-established meaning that excludes its reception by subjects who would interpret its salvific dimension for their lives, in the same way memory of the words spoken cannot be exercised outside subjects implicated in the weight of their state of suspense. The density of 'the subject' is not thrown out in the memorial of the Last Supper: the gift of salvation is inscribed in the flesh of subjects fully open in longing for openness to 'something other' than mercantile exchange. But we still need to place this longing for the gift, this Trinitarian desire, beyond the logic of the exchange mechanisms to which human beings too easily subscribe. In effect, if we restrict ourselves to what we see of the logic that rules the world, do we have the choice of reacting like the disciples? It needed Jesus' Word to short-circuit this worldly logic in order to make it possible to reach 'belief' in this deep longing in every human person, this longing for a gratuitous salvation. So Augustine sums up what takes place in the hearts of all those who live the mystery of the Eucharist: 'for we too have been made into his body, and, through his mercy, we are what we receive.'[5] *We* are created in the image of the Trinitarian God, and what *we* receive is this 'restored image' in *us*.

Conclusion

From the first to the second covenant, why do we still tell these stories? 'So that we may realize the depths from which we must cry to you.'[6] If Augustine so justified his 'Confessions', an account made for the 'we' to be formed in a cry toward God, it is also in this way that these accounts of loaves and gifts can be understood: so as finally to realize the depths from which the cry must arise, depths of hunger that weaken and kill, depths of longing for salvation deriving from the depths of the time recalled by the ritual of the covenant. Furthermore, this ritual places wine as heritage to be drunk only in the Kingdom of God, a kingdom in which it is not exchange, mercantilism, that rules, but giving, in a Trinitarian dynamic. This wine both quenches and produces thirst for God, the thirst for belonging to a kingdom in which the 'we' of belonging to the sons and daughters of God is formed, in response to the solitude anchored in a two-way mercantile exchange, engaged in a giving-giving process, without a third party to blast open that limited space, enclosed in unrelieved horizontality, with no prospects, in which the state of suspense can lead only to death, going down into which cannot produce the drive needed to climb out again.

The story of the Last Supper is retold down to the present in order to anchor the cry to God where we human beings are, in the distress of an anguished depth. We need to celebrate the Eucharist in order to speak out of this very particular state of suspense, a mixture of the hunger in which three quarters of humankind languish and our no less widely spread despair. The account aims to make those who read it descend into the depths and emerge again toward God, so that their cry does not stray into a false depth, a depth of compliance, a depth of pride in itself, a 'spectacle' depth. This is why the account becomes a duty toward one's sisters and brothers, to show, to give, to share the cry's journey to God. The Eucharist thereby seeks to transform the pain of the descent into a shared journey, so that human beings do not remain closed and blocked in the pain of the descent. The Eucharist aims to provide the necessities for the journey. Life is confused, the road to God is unclear, and this is why the Eucharist sets out a topography to guide us in our confusion, so that in its midst we can find a way to salvation.

This is why spilt blood has to be reinvested with a meaning other than violent death, so as not to remain blocked in a purely sacrificial logic. Jesus redefines blood, which in itself carries a charge of violence, illustrated in the parable of the murderous winegrowers, by setting it 'elsewhere' and 'later': it will not be drunk except elsewhere, in the Kingdom of God, in another time that retrospectively traverses temporality to come down to us today. It will be drunk only when it is 'new', emptied of its charge of death to take the openness of the Covenant into itself. The opening of a space of salvation in the midst of human contingencies, in the midst of hunger, in the midst of despair, in the midst of death, comes about through the gift of the word, the gift of bread, the gift of the Body and the Blood. If bread brings the space for the openness of the Covenant that redefines the spaces of our state of suspense, wine brings in the new time of the Kingdom that redefines backward our time of waiting for salvation.

The given bread and cup bear the memory of hunger, of death, of inheritance, of murder, and inscribe them in the infinite openness of the Covenant and the Kingdom, in the form of a Trinitarian mode of openness.

Translated by Paul Burns

Notes

1. Augustine, *The Trinity*.
2. Augustine, *De doctrina christiana*, II, I, 2.
3. Irene Rosier-Catach, *La parole efficace. Signe, rituel, sacré*, Paris 2004, p, 483: 'Separating the relationship to the thing from the relationship to another would be to distort Augustine's definition as understood by the medievals.'
4. 'What does it profit to say that Jesus came only in the flesh he took from Mary and not also to show that he came in my own flesh?' (Origen, *Homily on Genesis*, 3, 7).
5. J.-M.-R. Tillard, *Chair de l'Église, chair du Christ. Aux sources de l'ecclésiologie de communion*, Paris 1992, p. 57: 'What you receive, you are yourselves, by the grace by which you are redeemed.'
6. Augustine, *The Confessions*, II, 3, 5.

Bread and Cup: Word Given for a Time of Absence

Louis Panier

Sharing bread, sharing the word, sharing relationships: these themes spring quite readily to mind as expressions of the message of the Eucharist; they also express what we understand as guidelines left by Jesus to his disciples. As such, the Eucharist would tell of Jesus' presence to his disciples and the 'way of life' indicated by that.

All these themes are effectively evoked by the Eucharist, the founding act of gift of self, of sharing, and of life in common, but they still need to be expressed in order to understand what they enable us to say and think on the basis of the mystery of Christ and the Eucharist. In this contribution I propose to read one of the New Testament texts that recall the words spoken by Jesus in the course of the last meal with his disciples.[1] The 'institution narrative' appears in the three Synoptic Gospels and in the First Letter to the Corinthians. I propose to study it in this last text, to see how particularly Paul's discourse to the Corinthians distinguishes and dwells on the 'Lord's Supper' and the need to share and to observe the social rules governing the meal. What is at stake here is seeing in what way the 'Lord's Supper' differs from all other meals, and how at the same time it transforms the meaning of these and recalls a basis for them, something that Paul's addressees have apparently not noticed.

My approach will be to note as accurately as possible the manner in which the narrative says what it does say, and I shall try to see how this manner of writing, which conditions our manner of reading, provides theological reflection with a problem and a certain rationale. So I shall not be taking the accounts of the institution of the Eucharist as models implying an attitude to life in common and sharing but approaching them as instituting a rationale that may be at work in the practice of sharing.

The reflections that follow fit the pattern of discursive theology, worked out on the basis of an analysis of biblical narratives and their signifying organizations (or structures).[2]

I. Eating at home or sharing the supper?

Among the recommendations made by Paul[3] in 1 Corinthians 11 there is one that concerns the observance of the Lord's Supper. Not only do the Christians of Corinth seem, in their gatherings, to take their food in a disorderly and precipitate fashion (v. 21), but they are steeped in contempt for the Lord's Supper, and these two attitudes are linked. It is in this context that Paul recalls Jesus' last meal ('the night he was betrayed') and reiterates the words of institution that found the memorial of the Eucharist.

The misconception (this lack of discernment, which brings judgment on them: v. 29) with regard to what constitutes this bread and this wine, has serious consequences for the body itself. Not only are the Corinthians divided as a Church, as a body (vv. 18, 19: there are divisions – *schismata* – and factions – *aireses* – among them), but this division affects each one of them as individual bodies – desirous bodies, subject to the virtually instinctive need for food: they go ahead with their own meal without waiting for others, one is still hungry while another is drunk; the body is sick and infirm. How can their misconception of the 'Body' at the Lord's Supper lead their bodies to this passion-fuelled state of impulse and suspense, of disorder and de-structuration, of incoherence? If such are the consequences of misconstruing what is really involved in the Body proclaimed in the Eucharist, what can we suppose the significance of this Lord's Supper to be, if it is not a model of 'good behaviour in society' (since people had to eat at home before partaking in it), but can be what should establish the human significance of the shared meal for the Corinthians?

In this part of 1 Corinthians 11 Paul's discourse recalls a distinction that they apparently fail to appreciate, but it also stresses the effects of this failure: 'If you are hungry, eat at home' (v. 34). Does this mean that the Eucharist has nothing to do with a meal, with hunger, with the need to share, with rules for conduct in society (being a different occasion, in a different place, a different activity)? The Eucharist is undoubtedly not an alternative to the needs of everyday life, so it is appropriate to leave it in its significant difference, *because it is precisely this difference that is at stake*, the difference that establishes the link between food (body) and word, without which the word is lost in discourse and the body is wasted in its needs and excesses and in confusion. The Lord's Supper does not satisfy human hunger; it is a memorial and a proclamation, an act in word responding to Jesus' instituting word. Failing to appreciate the word and its body-effect produces loss of this cohesion: this word in action 'incorporates', 'constitutes-in-body', appeals to a body in order to be received.

II. The night he was betrayed

We now need to come back to this word of institution and to this account that has now come up against an obstacle in the excessive ways of the Christians at Corinth. Analysis of this account and of these words will enable us to look more closely at the elements in the preceding considerations.

This account has met an obstacle. This is effectively introduced fairly bluntly in the text: *'For I received from the Lord . . .'* (v. 23). Having described the attitude of the Corinthians ('you') on the basis of what he has 'heard' (v. 18), the speaker Paul ('I') opposes what he has *received* and what he has in turn *handed on*. The faulty attitude of the Corinthians stems from information (what is said and has come to Paul's ears), while the account of the institution itself stems from tradition: two different modalities of discourse, two distinct word-chains. Paul does not respond to the information he has received with moral considerations on what should be done to enable the food to be better shared among all. Faced with the unruly *attitude* of the Corinthians, he opposes an *event*, a founding one, the account of a meal at which the bread and cup are arranged in such a way that eating may be proclaiming, that eating may be an act of word – but at what cost?

If eating is thus to be no longer the habitual response to a famished body's needs but a singular event ('as often as') and a proclamation, this means that, on that night, in the event related, body, food, and word became fused in a unique and founding way. We should now try to develop this correlation, this fusion, by returning to the text, to the 'institution narrative'.

In 1 Corinthians, as in the Synoptic Gospels, the institution narrative comprises a discourse by Jesus, situated in the context of the last meal (or of the night he was betrayed). The elements of the meal are present in the narrative – the bread, the cup, those partaking – but the discourse re-designates them through a signification device, linked to Jesus' words and articulating a new relationship between Jesus' body and blood and the disciples. What I want to stress is this re-designation. Jesus' discourse consists of three sections: words over the bread and body, words over the cup and blood, and words instigating the memorial ('Do this, as often as you drink it'), with which Paul's statement in v. 26, 'For as often as you eat', connects.[4]

Using certain methodological elements of the semiotics of discourse here, we can try to describe some aspects characteristic of Jesus' words, and in particular to show the coherence of the sections and their relative function.

(a) Words over the bread

Jesus' words are placed in a context, in a referential situation: we have the bread, the cup, the partakers in the meal, and the moment of the last night. Within this context, Jesus' words are set in a series of actions: *taking the bread, giving thanks, breaking, giving, and saying*. These words form an act, an act of assertion that works to displace the device in place by installing a fresh device on the basis of a singular word-usage: 'I – here – now – this'.[5] The constituent elements of the meal are stated to be different through the process of the word that names them. Everything happens as though Jesus were introducing a 'fictional' world into the 'realistic' ensemble of the meal: bread-body, cup-blood of the Covenant: Jesus' form of words constitutes an assertion: 'this is'. This assertion constructs a metaphor *in praesentia* between the bread shown and designated ('this') and the body of the speaker present in his uttering of the word. But this word is also an address ('for you') that inserts the disciples into this new disposition.

In this way a new and fairly complex signifying device is constituted, of which certain dimensions can be set out:

1. *I / my* body / *this* bread: A signifying link is established: on the one hand between the bread and the word-process divided between the 'I' who speaks and the body of the speaker, a real link from which this word derives; on the other hand between the operations carried out on the bread (taking, blessing, breaking, giving) and the act of assertion carried out by the speaking and asserting subject. The originating setting of this assertion (from where the word comes, so to speak) becomes cut off, divided, or detached from itself: MY body (from which 'I' speak) in THIS bread (which is not 'me').[6]

2. Jesus' words instituting the Eucharist do not posit a simple symbolic relationship between bread and body, as between the signifier and signified of a sign. This linkage, brought about in the very act of speaking the words, concerns the very conditions of the discourse here addressed ('for you'). The assertive act itself seeks to become manifest, realized, in the figure of the body whose course (body given) is made homologous to that of the bread (broken, blessed, given). The correlation of bread to body is not a magical transformation of objects, it is a construction of meaning, which is established among real courses of events, that of the bread broken and given and

that of the body engaged in the act of speaking, courses in which the difference and separation kept between them refer back to the act of speaking that
produces them.

3. Jesus' formulation sets out the very conditions of the incarnate word (or
of the incarnation of the word), the conditions of significance. Engaged in
the act of speaking, the subject is divided by the significance. The bread,
throughout its course (until it is given and eaten), demonstrates – by its
'objectivity', its 'materiality', at a distance from the speaker, from the
linguistic components of his discourse, and even from the content of his
message – the break that defines 'MY-BODY' in the assertion of the word.
The bread is not the visible sign of an invisible body (especially in this
discourse when Jesus is present to his disciples:[8] they evidently have the
body and the bread before them!). It is the signifier of the break that marks,
in that it is the setting of the word, a body always lost/given. We have to
move through this otherness, through this bread and this wine and through
their difference, to manifest but also to bring into being a body proper to
(for) the word.

If this is the case, we are perhaps in a better position to understand the
distance separating this 'Lord's supper' from what the Corinthians had
managed to make of it. . . .

We can then put forward the hypothesis that the word spoken over the
bread articulates a 'law of assertion' (in the 'technical' sense of the term),
that is, it establishes in discourse and in operation the conditions for the
emergence of the act of speaking and of the speaking body.

(b) Words over the cup

What then can we say about the words over the cup? Do they form a simple
reprise of the formula, completing a stereotypical couplet of figures and by
their cleavage (bread / wine – body / blood) indicating at once a totality of
life and a mortal and sacrificial separation? It is possible to link the words
over the bread and the words over the cup in the light of the hypothesis
formulated above: while the bread put the initial conditions of the incarnate
word in place, the words over the cup develop the possibilities of the
discourse and of its deployment: it is a question of the figure and of its
fulfillment,[9] and this question is logically connected to the preceding one.

In fact, the words over the cup take up virtually the same narrative
elements of the words over the bread: the cup is here still the object that
designates the division between the subject and the assertion: this cup / my

blood; but here the cup is interpreted in the discourse: 'This cup is the new covenant in my blood'.[10] What can we say about this re-formulation?

Qualified in relation to the *covenant* and defined as *new*, this cup derives meaning from its relationship to an *old covenant*. A course between figures is thereby traced, a course of figures capable of linking a discourse, thereby marking a point of fulfillment.[11] Jesus' present assertion, whose conditions have just been spoken and signified by the words and action over the bread, fulfils the old covenant without invalidating it and so makes it into a *'figure'* of that which, here and now (at this meal, on the night he was betrayed) is brought about *in reality*. The covenant is fulfilled by what really happens here, but this reality, concerning as it does Jesus' body and its link to the words can only be 'figured' by these figures deriving from the Old Testament. Here again we are not in a symbolic sign device (signifier / signified) between the cup and the blood: the cup signifies the break that, in the Easter event, affects the actual body of Jesus and, not being able to be directly spoken or signified, can only be pointed to on the horizon of the play of figures, of their repetition, of their *reprise* in the expectation and perspective of a body to come. We shall see later how the announcement of this body is proclaimed and how it is just in the direction of this horizon that Paul re-states the narrative from tradition on the statement given in his letter (v. 26).

If the words over the bread place us in the initial conditions of the word, the words over the cup indicate the conditions for the significance of the discourse that this word deploys: of the meaning arrived at in the interplay of figures (old / new covenant) and in their separation.

(c) Memory of expectation

The third segment of Jesus' reported speech concerns memorial ('Do this, as often as you drink it, in remembrance of me'). In 1 Corinthians the institution narrative ends at this point, and Paul's discourse takes over once more.

On the level of assertion, it is interesting to see the precise interplay between the textual indices: the indications of the person and the temporal indices. In Jesus' discourse (v. 25) the pronoun 'you' refers to the disciples, the recipients of the words, of the bread, and of the cup. In v. 26, where Paul is speaking, the same pronoun 'you' refers to the recipients of the letter. There is thus an assertive syncretism at work, which 'actualizes' Jesus' speech and renders it operative (performative) in the 'present' situation.[12]

An assertive effect is also produced on temporality. The discourse introduces an iterative future in v. 25 ('as often as you drink it') and a retrospective temporality (memory) referred to Jesus' presence addressing his disciples on that particular night. In v. 26, where Paul is the speaker, there is also an iterative form, but this time in the present tense ('as often as you eat ... and drink') and a temporality, this time oriented toward the future ('until he comes'). The text thereby plays on the capacity of assertion to be situated in a non-chronological temporality, since the present is indexed to the act of speaking, and the personal indications (pronouns) relative to this act (particularly the 'you' here) designate nothing other than this position in relation to the word. Starting from the 'historical' moment of Jesus' assertion, well marked in the narrative form ('the night he was betrayed'), a particular temporal device is developed, which links together the still present assertive actions, between *memorial* and *proclamation*. In Paul's discourse, the proclamation then joins together the word-act and temporal situation ('until').

Jesus' actions and his words over the bread and the cup inaugurate *the time of the figure* for the disciples and also for the recipients of the letter; this is a limited time: by the present moment of Jesus' assertion (the night he was betrayed), the instant of the spoken word, but also the moment of his departure, absence, and death, on the one hand; by the moment (proclaimed but not fixed) of his coming again, on the other.[13] The period defined in this way takes its meaning from its relationship to the old covenant fulfilled in Jesus' action – and made into a *figure* to render it sayable. If the time of sacrament is opened in this way, it will be the time of waiting for him to come again, of a waiting proclaimed and enacted in the repetition of the meal.

This is, in my view, the position of the sacrament and its function as *incarnate* word, of memory and of expectation. On the basis of his position – 'I-here-now' – and of the word-event he brings about, Jesus' assertion projects: (a) a duration crowned and punctuated by a non-indefinite repetition, for a fixed term (do this, as often as you . . .); (b) a particular condition for the people to be born of this new link between word and body, in the expectation of a new body to come. The Lord's Supper of which Paul hands on the tradition concerns the body, the ecclesial body in its cohesion (threatened by 'schisms' and 'heresies'), and the individual body (stricken by sickness and infirmity), but it proclaims the body-to-come: failing to discern the body of the Lord, as the institution narrative records, means falling into insignificance, into confusing the bread and the cup with the needs of hunger and thirst, into confusing signifiers with things, figures in discourse with ideological messages (the divisions and factions of 1 Corinthians 8–9). It means discounting the separation that maintains the difference between body and word and speech, and which sustains the expectation of the Lord.

In Matthew, Mark, and Luke this temporal device is handled somewhat differently:[14] *'I will never again drink of the fruit of the vine until that day when I drink it new in the kingdom of God'*. We might be surprised to find the figure of the *product* – or fruit – of the vine (*genêma*) here replacing the figure of the cup. True, until now the narrative has used the cup, the figure of the blood, opening the figurative tour of the covenant. But here it is the product (fruit) of the vine that is to be drunk.[15] The cup is suddenly seen as it were emptied of its 'figured' meaning and now taken *a minima* in its more prosaic sense: it is not directly related to wine, nor is it now a matter of blood or of covenant . . . just the 'fruit of the vine'. The only remnant of this extreme figurative montage, in which the cup of the paschal meal can have been included in the run of figures of the covenant, is the fruit of the vine to drink . . . and it is in this prosaic figure (if indeed it is still a *figure?*) that the final fulfilment is spoken, the ordering of the repetition and restating of the figures. And while it is a matter of *drinking*, it is clearly a renewed body that is involved. . . . The cup is no longer 'symbolizable'; it is only to be 'drunk', and that by Jesus, in that future that is coming and is no longer the time of signs. Properly speaking, the fruit of the vine is no longer a 'figure' like the bread/body and the cup/blood (of the covenant); it no longer forms part of an interpretive device, but it touches and marks, as drink, that body which, in the act of asserting, becomes engaged (and lost) in the significance and in the order of discourse. The new drink witnesses to a re-found body and a shared existence; and we need to able to ask ourselves about the function of the place where these new conditions are established: the 'kingdom of God'.[16] If the signifying device I have been trying to describe has its origin in the 'I-here-now' of Jesus' words, it would be worth analyzing the new conditions of this event, where the actors (I + you), the time, and the place are differently disposed.

This brief study has sought to focus solely on the text of 1 Corinthians, on the way in which it introduces and cites the account of Jesus' last meal. Taken in the context of Paul's ongoing argument, in his quarrel with the practices of the Corinthians, the institution narrative does not come across as a simple model or example of sharing the bread and the word in assemblies; it rather seems to set the structural conditions for making people fit for the word-event that brings Jesus' paschal meal into being.

Translated by Paul Burns

Notes

1. An analysis of all the accounts is to appear (from L'Harmattan, Paris) under the title 'Le signe rompu du corps. Modèles sémiotiques et discours théologiques' in *Corps du signe / signes du corps. Actes du Symposium de Lyon, Septembre 2002.*

2. This approach is carried out by the Centre for Analysis of Religious Discourse (CADIR) at the Catholic University of Lyon. A methodological presentation and application of this practice, backed by a semiotic reading of the texts, can be found in L. Panier, *La Naissance du Fils de Dieu. Sémiotique et théologie discursive* (Cogitatio fidei 164), Paris 1991; Idem, *Le Péché Originel. Naissance de l'homme sauvé*, Paris 1996; F. Martin, *Pour une théologie de la lettre. L'inspiration des écritures* (Cogitatio fidei 166), Paris 1996. A. Fortin, 'Lire le geste théologique des écritures' in *Des théologies en mutation. Parcours et témoignages* (Acts of the 36th Canadian Theology Society Congress, Quebec 1999), Montreal 2002; Idem, 'Du sens à la signification: Pour une théorie de l'acte de lecture en théologie', *Laval théologique et philosophique* 52 (1996), pp. 327–38.

3. For convenience, I refer here to 'Paul' and 'Corinthians'. In the text of the epistle, 'Paul' and 'the Christians of Corinth', as historical personages, do not appear directly; they are 'represented' by 'enunciation marks' ('I', 'you'). In analyzing the text, we need to take care not to confuse the signification device constructed by the text of the epistle and the historical circumstances in which the message is communicated. It is of course on this condition that we can still situate ourselves as readers, 'enunciators' of a letter not addressed to us.

4. The enunciation marks are precise enough to distinguish the part formed by the account of the institution as a received discourse.

5. We can recognize here the characteristics of the process of enunciation as defined by the linguist E. Benveniste: every act of speaking defines a 'perspective centre', a 'presence', which seeks to indicate itself by means of the 'enunciation indices' made up particularly of personal pronouns, demonstrative adjectives, and verb tenses.

6. 'A sign is a body detached from the human body [. . .], the production of signs is an act of detachment [. . .]. Why do we have this "impulse" to de-multiply, by an act of detachment, the world of physical things into another world that is, also, made up of physical things, used as signs?' E. Güttgemans, 'La "différance" de la barre entre le corps et l'âme constituante du sens. Thèses sémiotiques' in CADIR, ed. L. Panier, *Le temps de la lecture. Mélanges offerts à Jean Delorme*, Paris n.d.

7. Cf E. Benveniste, 'Sémiologie de la langue' in *Problèmes de linguistique générale*, II, Paris 1974, pp. 43–66; F. Martin, 'Devenir des figures ou des figures au corps' in *Sémiotoque et Bible* 100 (2000), pp. 3–13.

8. It would also be interesting to follow the mentions of the body in the post-resurrection narratives. Cf L. Panier, 'Espace et Narrativité: le point de vue

d'un sémiotique discursive. Lecture de Jean 20' in *Sémiotique et Bible* 111 (2003), pp. 5–23.

9. Cf F. Martin, 'Parole, Écriture, Accomplissement dans l'Évangile de Matthieu' in *Sémiotique et Bible* 50–54 (1988–9); Idem, 'Devenir des figures', art. cit; Idem, 'La théorie des figures dans l'exégèse biblique ancienne. Résonnances sémiotiques' in *Sémiotique et Bible* 100 (2000), pp. 14–24.

10. Note that in the parallel narratives the cup is called 'this cup that is poured out for you [. . .] the new covenant in my blood' (Luke) and 'blood of the covenant, which is poured out for many' (Matthew, Mark).

11. This conception of figures and their fulfilment is taken from the propositions made by P. Beauchamp in *L'un et l'autre testament. Essai de lecture*, Paris 1976.

12. Note that this enunciative 'present' can convoke the readers of the letter also (including us) insofar as they enter into this enunciative contract. This present is equally operative in the liturgical tradition of the narrative and its re-citation in the Eucharistic liturgy. The enunciative device of the liturgy is furthermore fairly complex, as the institution narrative pronounced before the assembly (and in its name) is enounced by the celebrant (in the position of I), addressed to God (YOU) in prayer ('we give *you* thanks).

13. There is a similar temporal device in the parable of the pounds (Luke 19): the survey of trading of the pounds, initiated by the master on his departure, is bounded by his return – proclaimed but not fixed (v. 13), when the survey will be carried out. Cf L. Panier, 'Récit et figure dans la parabole des mines (Luc 19)' in *Modèles linguistiques* XXIV, 1 (2003), pp. 97–108.

14. This word is placed at the head of the text in Luke and at the end in the others.

15. The texts do not exactly speak of 'new wine'.

16. Here we need to detail the analysis of variants in the narrative: Matthew alone writes, 'until that day when I drink it new *with you* in *my Father's* kingdom'. Mark and Luke mention 'kingdom of God'. The texts develop a different tonality for this new occasion.

Christ, Eucharist and Human Hunger in the Theology of Augustine of Hippo

ROBERT DODARO, OSA

Augustine of Hippo (354–430) examines the relationship between Christ, the Eucharist, and human hunger in conjunction with his theology of 'the integral Christ' (*Christus totus, Christus integer*), a theme which stands at the centre of his reflection about Christ and the Church.[1] He develops this theme by combining the Pauline image of Christ as the bridegroom and the Church as the bride (Ephesians 5.32) with that of Christ as head of the body which is formed of members of his Church (Colossians 1.18–24).[2] Augustine's reflection upon these images coincides with his understanding of the incarnation as uniting Christ and his Church.[3] His initial interest in these Pauline images stems from their usefulness in enabling him to interpret numerous biblical passages in which Christ is the speaker. Such was the case with the Psalms, which were understood in early Christian tradition as the prayer of Christ. One of the difficulties for scriptural interpretation presented by this assumption is that not every verse of the Psalms seems appropriate to Christ, as for example, those passages in which the psalmist confesses sin. By employing the image of Christ as head of the body (*Christus caput corporis*) Augustine is able to identify Christ at times with his body, and at other times to distinguish between the two. He thus assumes that Christ is speaking at times on his own behalf, while at other times he speaks vicariously, on behalf of his body, the Church. By applying this principle to the biblical texts in question Augustine interprets certain scriptural passages as pertaining to Christ alone, others as pertaining to the members of his Church alone, and still others as pertaining to Christ and his Church together.[4] In this way Augustine understands Christ's pronouncement on the cross of the words of Psalm 22(21).1 'My God, my God, why have you forsaken me?' (Matthew 27.46), as Christ giving voice to the fear of death which he experiences vicariously on behalf of the members of his body. Similarly, when at Acts 9.4 Christ demands of Saul 'why are you persecuting me?', Augustine concludes that Christ is speaking on behalf of those members of his body who were the object of Saul's persecution.

The Presence of Christ

The exegetical principles which Augustine derives from the Pauline image of Christ as head of the body lead him to conclude that Christ and the Church are united by a close metaphysical bond founded in Christ's love for the members of his body. Augustine finds support for this conclusion in certain New Testament passages. For example, in the same verse in which Paul speaks of Christ as the bridegroom and the Church as the bride (Ephesians 5.32), the apostle describes this union as a mystery (*mysterion*), which Augustine translates *sacramentum magnum*. This passage, among others, leads him to conclude that the Pauline imagery linking Christ and his Church is more than metaphorical in its intent. The scriptures inform us, Augustine says in Sermon 341, that Christ is as real and present to us in the members of his body as he is in his being coeternal with the Father as the divine Word, or as the incarnate Christ, the son of Mary, who was crucified and died for us. In this sense, Augustine concludes, the church is the 'third mode' (*modus tertius*) of Christ's existence.[5] Augustine also places great importance on Paul's declaration at Philippians 2.6 that in becoming man, Christ took on the form of a slave. He interprets the image of Christ as 'slave' (*seruus*) in conjunction with his declaration at Matthew 25 '. . . when I was hungry you gave me to eat . . . what you did for the least of mine, you did for me', as indicating more than just a moral identification between Christ and the poor. Christ, for Augustine, is really present in the members of his body who stand in the deepest spiritual and material need.[6] Furthermore, drawing from his conclusions that as head of the body, Christ is united by love for his members, especially for those who suffer, Augustine concludes that Christ fully experiences in himself whatever suffering human beings feel, even the suffering that arises from human sinfulness. Augustine believes that as a consequence of his ability to give voice to the pain which members of his Church experience, Christ becomes the focal point for human suffering. He is therefore present in the hungry, the homeless, the imprisoned; in short, he is present in the most marginalized human beings throughout history.

Although Augustine understands the bond between Christ and his members as applying mainly to Christians who constitute the Church, he nevertheless includes the poor and hungry who are not Christians within his treatment of the 'integral Christ'.[7] Augustine does not generally apply the category of 'brothers and sisters' (*frater*) to non-Christians, because he finds that the New Testament restricts this title in a formal sense only to Christians.[8] Yet, against the exclusionary force of this designation, he emphasizes that the New Testament represents non-Christians as 'neighbours' (*proximus*), and he insists that, as neighbours, non-Christians should also be conceived as brothers and sisters, because all human beings are descendants of common parents, Adam and Eve.[9]

On the basis of charity

Several conclusions follow for Augustine from this analysis. First, Christ is present in the everyday experience of Christians as they encounter the poor in the streets and in the world. Augustine insists in his preaching that when Christians welcome the poor, the hungry, and the homeless into their midst and offer them food and shelter, it is Christ whom they really welcome and assist.[10] So strong for Augustine is Christ's self-identification in Matthew 25 with the hungry or poor in the midst of the Church that the care which Christians show to them becomes the main criterion for determining the character of their discipleship. He maintains, moreover, that Christians will be judged on the basis of the charity which they show toward the poor, more than by their practice of other virtues, or by their observance of other moral precepts.

> They may have been chaste, and not been given to fraud nor to drinking to excess; they may have abstained from evil deeds. But if they had not gone beyond that and done what Matthew 25 says, they would have remained quite barren. They would indeed have carried out the injunction, 'never yield to evil', but they would not have heeded what followed, 'practice good' (Ps 34(35):15). Christ does not say to these people, 'Come, receive the kingdom', for you have lived chastely, you have not practiced deceit or oppressed the poor, you have not trespassed on the rights of others or misled them by taking a false oath. It is not this that Christ says, but 'receive the kingdom, because I was hungry and you gave me to eat'. How greatly this compassion outweighs all the rest. For on every other matter the Lord is silent. He mentions this alone.[11]

Augustine reasons further that the love which unites Christ as head with all the members of his body similarly unites all the members with each other in such a way that 'the pain of one, even of the smallest member, is the pain of all'.[12]

Eucharist

The connection in Augustine's thought between the concept of the 'integral Christ', the material care for the hungry and the poor as urged by Matthew 25, and the Eucharist is most clearly developed in Augustine's treatment of Luke 24.13–35 (cf. Mark 16.12–13), the pericope of the disciples' encounter with the risen Lord on the road to Emmaus. Augustine preaches on this passage regularly during the octave week of Easter. In one of these sermons, he focuses on the Gospel verse in which the disciples are said to have recognized the Lord in the breaking of the bread (Luke 24.35). In recounting this encounter, Augustine stresses that before the disciples recognized that the stranger whom they met on the way was the risen Lord, they had welcomed him into their midst and showed him hospitality. Conscious as well that their companion was hungry, they had also invited him to share a meal with them. It was only when the stranger broke the bread and said the blessing, that the disciples recognized that he was in reality Christ.[13] For Augustine it is significant that this recognition took place in conjunction with the Eucharist. He views the Eucharistic breaking of bread as a sacrament, or sacred sign, in which Christians recognize in faith that what they do for the poor, hungry, and homeless, they do for Christ. Moreover, the Eucharist reminds them that in acting charitably toward the poor, they ought not to boast to themselves of their virtue. Augustine understands the Eucharist as the sacrifice by which Christ offers himself to the Father. As such it teaches Christians that whenever they offer something to God, it is they themselves who receive and are nourished in the offering.[14]

Augustine treats this latter point in some detail in his *City of God*. There he characterizes the Eucharist as a visible sacrifice in which the invisible sacrifice (compassion, mercy) which God desires of human beings is made manifest. In doing so, he returns to the concept of the 'integral Christ' and to the unity it establishes between Christ and members of his body. Augustine couples this image with another Pauline concept in which Jesus, 'though in the form of God, did not deem equality with God something to be grasped at, but emptied himself and took on the form of a servant' (Philippians 2.7).[15] Augustine suggests that as symbolic language, the Eucharist instructs believers that Christ, the true priest, offers in his death the one sacrifice that is acceptable to God.[16] Christ's sacrifice, therefore, also contains the invisible sacrifice that Christians, as members of his body, offer to God when they show compassion to their neighbour. As a consequence, Christians are reminded in the Eucharist that they should not esteem themselves for their virtuous deeds. Instead, Augustine argues, they should recognize that the source of their virtue is found not in themselves, but in Christ. By adopting this perspective, he maintains, they too assume the 'form of a servant', and in imitation of Christ, do not grasp at equality with God.[17]

In Sermon 239 Augustine insists that because Christ, through whom everything was created, could not have ever been in need, neither are the poor, hungry, and homeless, in whom Christ dwells, ever in real need.[18] In saying this, he does not underestimate the misery of material poverty, but contrasts it with the deeper spiritual misery which he believes is often experienced by those who are materially secure or well off. If God wills to do so, Augustine argues, he can provide for the physical needs of the poor, just as he provided for the physical needs of the prophet Elijah and of the widow from whom he begged food (cf 1 Kings 17). But God provides for the spiritual needs of believers by eliciting from them generosity and hospitality toward those who are in material need. It is by caring for the poor that those who are materially secure are spiritually nourished. Just as the widow, by generously giving the last of her remaining food to Elijah, received a longer life from God in return, Christians who offer solace and hospitality to the poor in their midst receive eternal life from God, Augustine argues.[19] In this way, he sees the Eucharist prefigured in the meal shared by Elijah and the widow. In this biblical narrative, as in the account of the disciples encountering Christ on the road to Emmaus, Augustine focuses on the Eucharist as the graced moment in which Christians come to recognize Christ in the hungry, the poor, and in strangers to whom they offer care and hospitality.

Notes

1. In general concerning this theme, see T. van Bavel, *Recherches sur la christologie de saint Augustin. L'humain et le divin dans le Christ d'après saint Augustin*, Fribourg, 1954); M. Reveillaud, 'Le Christ-Homme, tête de l'Église. Études d'ecclésiologie selon les *Enarrationes in Psalmos* d'Augustin', *Recherches Augustiniennes* 5 (1968), pp. 67–94 ; P. Borgomeo, *L'Église de ce temps dans la prédication de saint Augustin*, Paris, 1972, pp. 191–232 ; T. van Bavel and B. Bruning, 'Die Einheit des "Totus Christus" bei Augustinus', *Scientia augustiniana. Festschrift A. Zumkeller OSA zum 60. Geburtstag*, ed. C. Mayer, Würzburg, 1975, pp. 43–75; G. Remy, *Le Christ médiateur dans l'œuvre de saint Augustin*, vol 1, Lille-Paris, 1979, pp. 738–80; T. van Bavel, 'The «Christus Totus» Idea. A Forgotten Aspect of Augustine's Spirituality', in T. Finan and

V. Twomey (eds.), *Studies in Patristic Christology. Proceedings of the Third Maynooth Patristic Conference 1996*, Dublin, 1998, pp. 84–94.

2. See also Colossians 2.9–10; 1 Corinthians 12.12–31; Ephesians 4.13, 5.22–33; Galatians 3.27–29, all of which Augustine considered as authentic Pauline texts. For this theme, Augustine also depends on the Donatist theologian Tyconius' *Liber regularum* (386 C.E.). See K. Forster, 'Die ekklesiologische Bedeutung des corpus-Begriffes im Liber Regularum des Tyconius', *Münchener Theologische Zeitschrift* 7 (1956), pp. 173–183; G. Gaeta, 'Le «Regole» per l'interpretazione della Scrittura da Ticonio ad Agostino', *Annali di Storia dell'Esegesi* 4 (1987), pp. 109–18; C. Kannengiesser, 'Augustine and Tyconius. A Conflict of Christian Hermeneutics in Roman Africa', in P. Bright (ed.) *Augustine and the Bible*, Notre Dame, 1999, pp. 149–77.

3. See especially Augustine, *Sermo* 341.1; 341.11 (PL 39.1493; 1499–1500). *Sermo* 341 represents a shortened version of *Sermo Dolbeau* 22. See *Sermo Dolbeau* 22.2[1] (ed. F. Dolbeau, *Vingt-six sermons au peuple d'Afrique* (Paris, 1996), pp. 171–172); and ibid. 22.19[11] (ibid., pp. 188–190). Augustine's sermons (*sermones ad populum*) are fully translated into Spanish, Italian, and English, and translations in German and Dutch are currently in progress.

4. See M. Fiedrowicz, *Psalmus vox totius Christi. Studien zu Augustins «Enarrationes in Psalmos»*, Freiburg, 1997.

5. See reference above, n. 3.

6. See T. van Bavel, *Augustinus, Van liefde en vriendschap* (Kampen, ²1986; Baarn, 1970) = *Christ in dieser Welt. Augustinus zu Fragen seiner und unserer Zeit*, Würzburg, 1974, = *Christians in the World*, New York, 1980. See also, idem, 'L'option pour les pauvres chez Augustin', *Collationes* 21 (1991), pp. 73–88. Augustine admits that among all the passages of scripture, it is this one which moves him the most. See Augustine, *Sermo* 389.4 (cf. *Revue Bénédictine* 58 (1948), p. 49): '. . . quod me fateor in scriptura Dei plurimum movit . . .'.

7. See especially Canning, *The Unity*, op. cit., p. 387–94.

8. See Augustine, *Enarrationes in Psalmos* 32.2.2.29, citing 1 Corinthians 7.15; Romans 14.10; 1 Corinthians 6.8. See also R. Dodaro, 'Frater', in C. Mayer, *Augustinus-Lexikon*, vol. 3, Basel, 2004ff., cc. 60–64.

9. See Canning, *The Unity*, op. cit., p. 389, citing Augustine, *De disciplina christiana* 3.3 (cf. 8.8). At p. 398 n. 199, Canning indicates other Augustinian texts in support of this conclusion.

10. See, for example, Augustine, *Sermones* 236 and 239.

11. See Augustine, *Sermo* 389.4–5 (cf. *Revue Bénédictine* 58 (1948), pp. 49–50).

12. See R. Canning, *The Unity of Love for God and Neighbour in St. Augustine*, Heverlee-Leuven, 1993,, p. 385, citing Augustine, *Sermo Denis* 19.5. Canning's treatment (pp. 331–420) of the *Christus totus* theme in Augustine in conjunction with Mt 25 is admirable for its breadth and clarity.

13. See Augustine, *Sermo* 239.2.

14. See Augustine, *Sermo* 239.4.
15. See Augustine, *De ciuitate dei* 10.6. See also *en. Ps.* 30.2.1.3, a key text in this discussion, one in which Augustine also indicates that Christ unites believers with his body which has assumed the 'form of a servant'. See B. Studer, 'Das Opfer Christi nach Augustins in G. Békés and G. Farnedi (eds) *De Civitate Dei X,5–6'*, *Lex orandi – lex credendi, Miscellanea P. Vagaggini,*, Rome, 1980, pp. 93–107, and the discussion by A. Verwilghen, *Christologie et spiritualité selon saint Augustin. L'hymne aux Philippiens*, Paris, 1985, pp. 269–84.
16. See Augustine, *De ciuitate dei* 10.20.
17. See Augustine, *De ciuitate dei* 10.6.
18. See Augustine, *Sermo* 239.4; cf. 239.6.
19. See Augustine, *Sermo* 239.3.

III. Bread and Belonging

Hunger for Bread – the Desire of the Other

Hadwig Ana Maria Müller

Hunger and desire are part and parcel of human life . . .

I speak about the hunger which can be satisfied through eating, and about the desire which, triggered through an encounter with another human being, will increase by being in relation. Hunger is constitutive for human life as it is a dynamic entity which can be compared to an engine coming to a halt once its fuel is used up. Hunger constitutes an essential characteristic of human life: 'not without bread'. Desire is constitutive for human life as it is a social entity which can be compared to a network in which human beings are connected with each other through multiple human relationships. Desire constitutes the other essential characteristic of human life: 'not without others'.

The reality of desire is complex. It expresses the constitutive presence of others in my life, with potential wanting or suffering owing to the absence of others as an essential aspect. And it signifies inner and outer dynamics which aim to generate relationships with others in which this constitutive wanting 'not without others' is given a name and a face. Through this the experience of wanting might be experienced as more concrete, deeper, more painful, but also as a potential source of heightened joy or pleasure.

The desire about which I am speaking here is the 'desire of the other'[1] in both senses of the word. It is not only the desire which is aimed at the other but also that which comes from her or him. The other is not merely its object but at once and primarily its subject. Hence it is not fulfilled or 'satisfied' in a relationship with the other but it is awakened and increased all the more.

Hunger and desire: twice the urgent search for the 'other': for bread, for another human being; twice – figuratively speaking – hands reaching out, twice a deficiency which can be expressed in a request, twice a want which is 'radical' as it touches the very roots of human life. Human life cannot be thought about without hunger and desire. Both are the very definition of that which is our life in its neediness and fragility, in its openness and beauty.

. . . in radically different ways

Hunger and desire are essential aspects of human life – but, and this has to be pointed out, in radically different ways. Hunger is part of life as a want which has to be alleviated and eradicated. The bread itself is relief for the want not to be able to live without bread. Desire on the other hand is part and parcel of human life as a want which cannot really be alleviated or eradicated. In no way does the other reduce this fundamental condition of our lives, not to be able to live without her or him. On the contrary: she or he is the constant presence of this condition, she or he brings it into force.

Hunger limits life. The expectation and the joy of one who is hungry are in the satisfaction of the hunger. Hunger should not even begin to happen and even less it should persist or become chronic. The desire for the other on the other hand generates life. In the want expressed by it the other is present! Therefore there is no real easing of the desire; if its motion came to a halt life itself would stop. The point is to keep the desire alive and to deepen it. On the other hand it can also be covered up, suppressed or denied.

To satisfy hunger means to 'eat', and that means: to destroy that at which the hunger is aimed: 'to take nourishment into oneself'. To keep desire alive however requires the opposite. If desire is the want which the other creates within me it is all the more important that she or he exists. With regard to desire the point is therefore not the destruction through absorbing of the other but to respect, protect and affirm the other in her or his existence which is separate and distinct from mine.

Satisfying hunger – keeping desire alive: an impossible hierarchy

Bread and relationship – at first sight the order of their aims, described the search of 'hunger' and desire, appears to be obvious: the primary objective is bread, and after that relationships and the joys and pains connected with giving space to the desire.

On closer reflection however I am not really able to establish a clear, unchangeable and universally valid hierarchy between the certainty of not suffering hunger, and the uncertainty of a life determined by the desire of the other. I am convinced that the two are interdependent. The assurance to have bread for this day and the next day which satisfies hunger is the foundation for relationships of peace and liberty; at the same time however relationships in which human beings respect each other as others and find each other desirable and in which their desire keeps the dynamic of mutual forgiveness and liberation alive is the foundation for having bread in the first place! One dependency cannot be expressed without the other.

For this conviction I can refer to personal experience.[2] The north-east of Brazil is an area plagued not only by times of drought. The unjust distribution of the land is the primary cause for the suffering of human beings and animals. Many of the families I know there are frightfully familiar with hunger and with the fear of hunger. And yet, at those times when they can enjoy a harvest, their primary concern is not for eating but for being able to share with others. For them, who frequently do not know what they will have to eat in the next few days, relationships are a primary concern! Thus the sharing of the fruits of the harvest becomes a feast in which all can participate so that the bread does not become less as it is shared. Something like the miraculous multiplication of bread takes place.

If we who live in the wealthy northern hemisphere do not anticipate that those who live in incredible poverty are prepared to offer such royal liberty of sharing, if we are surprised by it – and maybe even humbly astonished – how extraordinarily capable they are of living in relationships, this is only an indication that we ourselves do not have such liberty to share or such ability to relate to others. And yet the hunger among most of us can be satisfied. While even in our part of the world there are more and more people who can no longer take their daily bread for granted, we cannot deny that poverty of relationships in our part of the world is greater than the want for bread. When Lula became president of Brazil he descried his aims as follows: 'My dream will become reality: that every man and woman in Brazil should have three square meals a day to satisfy their hunger.' Maybe it is not impossible to translate this dream for the reality of those of us living in Germany as follows: 'Every woman and man in Germany should listen to her or his desire at least three times a day and delight on relationships with others, the want for which she or he finds in her or his desire.'

Without a doubt bread secures the basis for living in peace and liberty – but the ability to find happiness in relationships includes the ability to share, and sharing seems to me to be the only way to satisfy hunger.

The satisfaction of hunger is a matter of relationships

The poor in Brazil have taught me: hunger is satisfied where human beings share with each other! The declaration of the Lula government that the majority of the Brazilian population who is used to hunger should have enough to eat generated a large number of initiatives and coalitions. They were all meant to be step in the same direction: re-distribution, a more just distribution of the goods of the land. The sheer size of the project however makes it very easy to forget that there is not distribution without sharing with each other, and this can only happen through concrete subjects. Only individuals and groups can share with each other; and this seems to be the only way for hunger to be satisfied in a way that will last.

We cannot take it for granted that human beings will share with each other. It requires that they enter into relationships with each other, that they visit each other, that they meet each other face to face. It requires hat they are patient with each other, in order to hear the true meaning of the silence and the stammering of the one and the fast speech of the other. That they take time to let their relationships grow: that they tame each other! That they take the risk to become vulnerable to the strangeness, the disturbing differences of the other! That they dare to offer the gift of faith to each other. That they are surprised by their respective beauty and the laughter of their hearts. That they allow themselves to discover that that they are attracted to each other. That they ask what the consequences of their friendship will have to be. That they suffer from their powerlessness and from the abyss that separates them. That they stay with each other and share their gifts.

Where does such sharing take place, such entering into relationships between the poor and the rich, between north and south, between those at the centre of society and those on the margins of the same society, between those who walk in darkness and those in the light? In many places, and through many people[3] – even if they are still very few in number compared to the masses of those who suffer from hunger. What is it that drives those few? Their desire! A want that sends them searching, a lack that makes them aware of their poverty. They approach others not as rich people who have something to give but as those who are poor and want to receive from others. They do not suppress their search for relationships, they keep alive their desire, the hunger, within them.

Living in relationships is matter of 'hunger'

In this context I use 'hunger' in the figurative sense of the word. Desire for the other is concerned with the voice of need within us, the voice of our peculiar dependency: 'not without others'.

No human being at any time can exist for themselves. We move in relationships with others who are always already there before we are. We are seen before we are able to see ourselves. We are the subject of the conversation of others before we ourselves are able to speak. Who are we ourselves, independent from those with whom we are inseparably connected? We do not know! What we do know is that we are not fully represented in the image, the description which we or others can give of ourselves. That we are further ahead or not as far ahead at all, in any case in motion, not to be pinned down by whatever idea. That we are in the progress of becoming, and that we are so in relationship with others. What we know about ourselves like the precious source of our uniqueness is a mysterious somewhere else in relation to the here and now of what we ourselves and others say about us. This 'somewhere else' is realized in the desire of others, in the fact that we seek to 'arrive' time and time again in relationships.

The somewhere else of the subject, her or his want of being-there or, positively speaking; her or his excess of becoming and movement and the desire for the other is characteristic of human existence as such. True, we can deny our 'want' and our desire. We can pretend that we are those who we imagine to be or those whom others imagine us to be, as we are no longer in the process of becoming and arriving, as if there was no future, no movement. However, all this massive labour of denial would not change the profound truth of want or desire.

How can we listen to our own truth which always eludes us? How can we listen to the voice of the other who in her or his otherness can be pinned down or tied up, expressed or reduced to one image as our own truth, the other who herself wants and seeks to arrive in relation to me? This is where 'hunger' comes into play. This about becoming empty. A letting go of images and concepts which tempt us to keep the truth about the other within what is conceivable or can be imagined. Doing without any form of knowing in advance that which is certain. The point is to create an openness for unexpected and unpredictable encounters with the somewhere else of our own truth as well as the incomprehensible otherness of the other. This includes readiness to be exposed to this otherness as if unarmed, to make ourselves touachable and vulnerable but also to receive the generosity of others.

For a life in abundance

Then 'hunger' can be turned into the most wasteful feast, the gifts that are being shared can exceed by far what could possibly be received, and such surprises increase the 'hunger' not so much in the sense of a painful asceticism but in the sense of looking forward, of expectation. Such encounters are like acts of creation, they generate new life. In future our desire is aimed at actively promoting the irreducible otherness of the other and make our own contribution so that she or he may be seen more clearly in the mystery of her or his own otherness. The emerging otherness of the other deepens our desire. It is lived in a movement that never stops, that is inscribed in the entire duration of a lifetime.

As a 'matter of hunger' desire is therefore constitutive of life! The more we listen to the voice of our want, the more we are alive. Through listening to our desire we recognize that we ourselves have not yet arrived in the image and the word which represent us. These can only be seen or heard as a promise, as a pointer towards a future that can only be imagined. Such recognition of the arrival as those who we are which still awaits us forms the basis for life in community. The absence of that which we are in everything which we pretend or claim to be keeps us and our relationships moving. Our antennae for this absence, this wanting, for the desire of the other are precious. They are the decisive factor with regard to if and with what joy we become more and more ourselves, with regard to if and with what quality we live! The desire for the other not only sustains life but also with every surprise through the otherness of the other generates new life.

Perhaps we can say: as little as real life can exist where there is always hunger – as little can real life exist where human beings suppress the desire of the other. For it is indeed possible to deny desire and to lock ourselves into those images and concepts which we deem to have of ourselves and others. On the outside life goes on. But within us, this means death – just as it means death to deny one's hunger.

Bread and relationships, the extinction of hunger and the awakening and deepening of desire for the other serve life itself: a human life the promise of which is abundance (John 10.10). 'Life in abundance' is nothing other than 'life in community'. Life in community is 'life in abundance' as it is constantly renewed and increased, surrendered and in doing that multiplied.

Translated by Natalie K. Watson

Notes

1. My reflections on the topic of desire have been influenced by Jacques Lacan and his interpretation of Freud. See Jacques Lacan, *Écrits*, Paris, 1966.
2. After ten years of living and working with others in Brazil I had the opportunity to reflect theologically on the experiences of these years. See H. Müller, *Stärke*

der Armen – Stärke Gottes (Strength of the Poor – Strength of God), Mainz, 1998.

3. In this context I want to mention the World Social Forum which as I am writing this is meeting once again in Porto Alegre. Many of those who participate are 'bridge people' who are able to create relationships across cultural, economic and social divides and to enter into dialogue and exchange.

Women/Hunger/Bread

Joel Marie Cabrita

I. A cauldron of illicit loves

In Africa, due to famine, war and the ravages of AIDS, women are selling
their bodies for food, for themselves and for others. In the northern hemisphere world of abundant and cheap food, women are voluntarily starving
themselves to death. Equally, there are women who are obsessed with the
desire to consume their bread, but once having done so, are compelled to rid
themselves of it. There are also women who gorge: who stuff themselves on
the cheap breads, pasta, meats and cakes which the western world allows us
to do.

What does this mean for Christian reflection that has at its centre the act
of eating and drinking, the ingestion of Christ's bread and blood in the
Eucharist? In a female culture that is so uniformly and deeply ambiguous
about 'being fed', and all that this implies, how is the Christian sacrament of
receiving nourishment to be understood, and what is more, how can it be
constructively employed in the situation? Furthermore, how can Western
women understand themselves in solidarity with women elsewhere in the
world who are truly malnourished, in the most physical sense of the word?

The fourth-century theologian Augustine suggests that the basic dynamic
of human life is desire. It is desire which moves us towards any given end,
and it is desire that will finally move us towards God. All human error is
misplaced desire, wrongly directed desire, and grace consists in Christ
re-orientating our desire towards its proper end. This experience of chaotic
desire is one that resounds with women suffering from eating disorders.
Caroline Knapp, in her autobiographical memoir detailing her recovery
from anorexia, writes of her splintered appetites that her 'body was experienced as dangerous and disturbing and wrong, its hungers split off from
each other, each one assigned multiple and contradictory meanings, each
one loaded and fraught.'[1]

A woman's experience with her appetite is *loss* of her appetite, even when
she eats compulsively. Her loss is in her inability to read her hunger and to

interpret 'correctly' for what she hungers. Her hunger instead becomes a foreign and fearful language that may spell her doom. Compulsive action – whether of gorging or of starvation – becomes the blanket response to desire and need. Either we eat so much that our desire is squashed into a doughy and silent death, or we police our desire so rigidly that it is never has the chance to voice itself but is instead circumscribed in a daily diet of 'one plain sesame bagel for breakfast, one container of Danone coffee-flavoured yogurt for lunch, one apple and a one-inch cube of cheese for dinner.' This was Knapp's daily food for three years. Surely this confusion is also that of Augustine, who writes in his *Confessions* that he seethes amidst a rich and soupy 'cauldron of illicit loves . . . seeking an object for my love'[2], yet mistaken about what he hungers for. 'My hunger was internal, deprived of internal food, of God. But that was not the kind of hunger I felt . . . (my soul) thrust itself to outward things.' The motif for Augustine is that of ambiguity and obfuscation: hungers that conflict, hungers that are not appropriately voiced or translated, a hunger the source of which is hidden from his understanding.

The pivotal question is, of course: what do women desire? And why is it so hard for women to decode their desires, and why is it that the act of either excessive eating or of starvation becomes a shorthand for all desire, no matter if the desires be for life, love, liberation or literacy? The feminist dimensions of contemporary female obsession with food have been well documented. Susie Orbach, in 1982, writes that *Fat is a Feminist Issue*[3] and argues that for twentieth-century women food becomes a way to try and nurture themselves in an environment where female nurturance is a decidedly low priority. Food, standing as a complex symbol for the safety that is often denied to women, becomes the comprehensive means to appropriate the power, warmth and care that a women is so often called to dispense to others, and never to herself. However, this combines explosively with a pervasive culture of 'Beauty Myth' (a la Naomi Wolf[4]) that argues that as women increasingly make strides into hitherto male realms of business, academia, politics and government there is a corresponding clamp down on female self image. The more powerful women become in public life, the more violent is the pressure to conform to a waif-like and idealized representation of female beauty. A male-dominated advertising industry keeps perfect step with the public emancipation of women: as women become more powerful, they are encouraged to become smaller and smaller. Women may be edging men out of jobs, but they are being simultaneously physically and psychologically diminished – one can never be 'too thin'.

Thus to inquire into Western female hunger is to uncover a messy site of power play. Women are not only faced with Augustine's dilemma – original sin has perverted the appropriate direction of desire – but also with all the corresponding cultural 'corruptions' of desire. Female desire, in a Lacanian sense, has been removed from its own agency; it no longer dictates its own object but is addressed to simulacra upon simulacra of shadowy desired object that perpetually retreats beyond reach. We desire to be fed. We desire to feed others at our own expense. We desire to be thin. We desire to be thin because men desire us to be thin. We hunger for nourishment. We are compelled to forego nourishment. We desire food. We desire food because we desire more than food . . . These desires are refracted through the desires of others and the desires that we dare not voice: 'our life was one of being seduced and seducing, being deceived and deceiving, in a variety of desires.'[5]

II. Towards voicing hunger.

Ignatius of Loyola appears an unlikely dialogue partner in deciphering female hunger. The difficulties his *Spiritual Exercises* and their accompanying symbolism pose for women are manifold. Not only are female examples given as the inevitable negative 'type', but Ignatius' examples are also unswervingly patriarchal and his commitment to a Church that at times has been singularly destructive to woman's personhood is clear. Nonetheless, the Ignatian *Exercises* arguably provide a rich resource in naming and listening to female desire. The *Spiritual Exercises* offer a means to befriend and understand the complex, and often contrary, movements of the inner life of women and men. The Preface to the *Exercises* 'The First Principle and Foundation' opens by stating that

> Man is created to praise, reverence and serve God, our Lord, and by this means to save his soul. The other things on the face of the earth are created for man, to help him in attaining the end for which he is created. Hence, man is to make use of them in so far as they help him in the attainment of his end, and he must rid himself of them in so far as they prove a hindrance to him . . . our one desire and choice should be what is more conducive to the end for which we are created.

Ignatius, in an Augustinian manner, establishes our fundamental human orientation by means of desire. At our very deepest level we are directed in desire towards God, and this will be the means by which we save our souls.

The Ignatian work thus consists in a complex and nuanced series of 'discernments' of our desires. We work from the fundamental premise that the deepest desire of our soul is for God, and when we try to satisfy ourselves with something that is not leading us to God, we invariably feel empty, dry, depressed or bored. The woman following the exercises is challenged to read her desires: what desires are giving her joy, and what desires are diminishing her joy? The startling premise in all of this is this: that she can trust that her *true* desire – the desire that brings her lasting peace and joy – is in fact the desire for God.

A woman's inner life becomes sacramental; and it is this that is the great resource of Ignatius for hungry women. The desires of the soul – both painful and peaceful – are nothing other than the path to God. 'Man is to make use of (the things of this world) insofar as they help him in the attainment of his end.' The Ignatian God is not abstracted nor disembodied but rather comes incarnated within the daily matter of life. And most of all, in the substance of the inner life are the endless movements and desires of the soul that bear the trace of God. *The kingdom of heaven is within you* . . . To discover the divinity in our humanity, to see the soul as sacrament, is to realize a God who is present in all things and for whom all creation becomes sign of divine presence. Desire is divine trace rather than illicit love; correctly interpreted, it is that which will 'save our souls' when turned towards praise of God.

This is surely also the point of the culmination of the Ignatian *Exercises*, the *contemplatio ad amorem*, the 'Contemplation towards Love'. Here the first principle of the direction of desire– that we are created to praise, reverence and serve God and by this means to save our soul – is illuminated by the principle of love. Ignatius uses the language of giving and reception to describe this:

> Take, Lord, and receive all my liberty, my memory, my understanding and my entire will – all that I have and call my own. You have given it to me. To you, Lord, I return it. Everything is yours; do with it what you will. Give me only your love and your grace. That is enough for me.[6]

The notion of taking and receiving from God is nothing other than the movement of desire as love. We give ourselves in love to God, recognizing that God is the deepest desire of our heart; equally, we are able to receive the divine presence in all things. God's love is available to us in all creation – in plants, creatures and our own souls – and 'descend from above as the rays of light descend from the sun, and as the waters flow from their fountains.'[7] God's indwelling is grasped in all things, and it is the Ignatian way to find this presence not only in times of prayer, but in all things of our body and soul, joyful and painful alike.

This reconciliation of the life of the spirit with the life of the body is also the lesson of the eucharistic feast, and in the case of disordered eating, a particularly poignant lesson. For the Eucharist, the sacrament par excellence, the fruit of the vine and the grain of the field becomes the stuff of the divine, and it is here that physical and spiritual hunger perfectly coincide. Physical hunger – the human need to ingest bread and liquid – is read also as spiritual hunger: it is this bread and wine that also will nourish our soul.

Not only is the Eucharist the culmination of 'finding God in all things', but it also serves as a reminder of the mutuality of loving desire. Just as the 'contemplation towards Love' focuses on the reciprocity of giving and receiving, so does the Eucharist illuminate this cyclical movement. Bread and wine are given by Christ to the Body, broken for its sake, received in gratitude, then in time given again in the deeds of love. That desire is ultimately relational is an important lesson for women, particularly women suffering from eating disorders. To learn that female desire can be 'held' or met by an appropriate reception is a powerful affirmation of need, and is perhaps also the means to redeem the *cultural* fragmentation of female desire. The feminine voice has been repeatedly met with disinterest, rejection and silencing; desires are dismissed or refracted onto displaced objects ('its hungers split off from one another'). The Eucharist, as well as the Ignatian 'contemplation towards love', teach women to experience the dialogue of desire: an ongoing conversation of both giving and receiving, affirming and being affirmed in life.

III. Ceaseless hunger

Is this all to say that the Eucharist can be proposed as a 'template' for healing from disordered eating; that there is a 'Christian' solution to this cultural malaise? This brief piece in no way intends to present the Eucharist as an unambiguous symbol of correct desire. For the Eucharist – like all else that belongs, at least partially, to the natural world – is itself migratory, it is itself always continually pointing beyond itself. If Ignatius' principle of 'finding God in all things' is taken as a guiding principle to interpreting the world, then the implication is that things will always reveal themselves to mean more than they appear to. This is the restlessness of material objects, their continual traversing of themselves towards something yet unseen, unheard, unsatisfied. And it is precisely this restlessness that constitutes the sacramentality, or the 'doubleness' of the material: they never coincide with themselves, are always reaching beyond and excessive to themselves. It is this that challenges the satiety of Hegel's infinite: the Hegelian synthesis of the belly that is full, the hunger that is forever stilled. Rather, it is the sacrament that invites us beyond gluttedness, into and towards a forever receding object of desire.

So the challenge is to allow the Eucharist itself to speak of this very restlessness, and to not allow the false satisfaction of a Hegelian stasis, the state of complete stupefaction. This means letting the imperfections and failures of the Eucharistic sacrament to express themselves, to courageously allow its wounded doubleness to speak. One such thing that would emerge is the manner in which, although the Eucharist points us towards the possibility of genuine listening to female desire, it nonetheless has been used in achieving precisely the opposite ends. The issue of who is permitted to consecrate the Eucharist – never women – surely reminds us of the dangers of identifying any material object as an absolute end. The meaning of the Eucharist is that God is in all things. God in all things compels us towards doubleness; things reveal more of themselves than is first apparent. This, incidentally, is the error of the woman who is addicted to food or the denial of food: food in itself becomes the absolute end; creation is confused with the Creator; 'our life was one of being seduced and seducing, being deceived and deceiving, in a variety of desires.'[8]

The lies of seduction and deception will also arise when Western women, struggling with self-feeding problems, begin to come into conversation with women in the majority world. The problem displays radically different forms: one set of women are chaotically disordered amidst a superabundance of food; another set struggle to feed their families and, perhaps lastly, themselves. One problem is 'psychological', another economic and political. Yet there are pervasive similarities beneath this. Women in both contexts are dying of malnutrition; women in both the wealthy West and the rest of the world struggle with obesity as cheap refined carbohydrates flood both markets; paradoxically, Brazil has just diagnosed obesity as one of its most significant health threats, the USA's skyrocketing obesity rates are labeled 'malnutrition'. Is it perhaps not so simple to delineate the political and the psychological? I suggest that the chaotic desire of Western women cannot be understood separately from a context of capital and compulsive market consumption which itself mistakes the creation for the Creator. The

West's desire itself is disordered, saturated with goods it neither truly wants nor needs, its public sense of want is in crisis and bloated almost beyond recognition. Yet its crisis of desire affects the rest of the world: the rampant feeding of one part leaves the rest of the global body emaciated. It appears that a misdirection of desire is occurring on a global scale – that Western women's epidemic of eating disorders is but symptomatic of the illness of the whole body. The woman who alternately starves, gorges and purges herself of food is a miniature enactment of an macrocosmic disorder of desire.

To turn instead to the 'restless' Eucharist is not to denigrate the sacrament. Rather, it is a recognition that our ultimate object of desire is God, and we only know this God through the things of this earth, and that those things are on a continual pilgrimage. Objects continually reveal their hidden depths in an unending refractive process; this happening even in the most holy of objects. The Eucharist's deferral, which we see most starkly in its failure to hold female desire, is also found, more positively perhaps, in its non-equation with itself: bread is flesh, wine is blood. The deferral, or excessiveness, that characterizes the sacrament becomes life-giving, and displacement is generative of new life. This is Ignatius' lesson: to recognize reality's continuously dynamic character, never to equate a given situation with the depth of its truth, and to appreciate continually the excessive in the ordinary, 'God in all things'. This is as true for any given political reality as it is for the inner cartography of our souls; to allow a capitalist world economics to question and 'exceed' itself. Indeed, this perpetual 'pointage' action is reminiscent of the inner life of the Trinity; a superabundant and perpetual overflowing of the limits of the given.

Something of this same excessiveness is at work in disordered female eating, and the refracted desires it is symptomatic of. The movement of desires being perpetually deferred onto 'inaccurate' objects is surely part of what it means to be material, even when this is deeply painful. The work of recent feminist psychoanalysts suggests that it is not entirely appropriate to label negative eating experiences as 'disordered'. Instead, so they suggest, they are merely symptomatic of the endless and human work of deferring desires. When the world around us is unable to be receptive to female need, they are nonetheless other receptacles of desire. Self-feeding, or self-starvation, becomes for a time the best a woman can do. Again, and particularly poignantly here, this desire is never entirely met, endlessly restless it seeks for a better resting place. 'My heart was restless until it found its rest in You'. Startlingly, we find that the lesson of the Eucharist for women in the grip of food obsessions is a gentle one, and one that Ignatius would recognize: watch the drift of these desires, recognize that they always continually transform both themselves and their object, embrace the double message of all human desire, and finally at the end, rest in the perpetual play of the Trinitarian life that the Sacrament speaks to us of so persistently.

Notes

1. Caroline Knapp, *Appetites : why women want.*, New York, Counterpoint, 2003, p. 1.
2. *Confessions* III, I, 1.
3. Susie Orbach, *Fat is a Feminist Issue*, London, Paddington Press, 1978.
4. Naomi Wolf, *The Beauty Myth: How Images of Beauty Are Used Against Women*, London, Vintage, 1991.
5. *Confessions*, IV, I,1.
6. *Spiritual Exercises*, Paragraph 234.
7. *Spiritual Exercises*, Paragraph 237.
8. *Confessions*, IV, I,1.

Consumption, the Market, and the Eucharist

William T. Cavanaugh

There was a woman named Rosalinda with whom I attended Sunday mass when I lived in Chile in the 1980s. Rosalinda lived in a small wooden shanty with her elderly mother. Their income, which sufficed for little more than bread and tea, was derived from the potholders and other items that Rosalinda crocheted and sold at the local market. On one of my first visits to her home, Rosalinda gave me a little crocheted bird that is used for grasping the handles of hot tea kettles. When Rosalinda presented it to me as I was leaving her home, my first impulse was to reach into my pocket and give her some money for it. But I sensed that that would have been the wrong thing to do.

The little blue-green bird with a white fringe currently adorns the rice container on my kitchen counter. I live with my wife and kids a world away from Santiago in St. Paul, Minnesota. We live our lives at the intersection of two stories about the world: the Eucharist and the market. Both tell stories of hunger and consumption, of exchanges and gifts. The stories both overlap and compete. I will try to tell these two stories briefly, and reflect on what they mean for Rosalinda and the bird.

I. Hunger and the market

Economics, we are told, is the science which studies the allocation of resources under conditions of scarcity. The very basis of the market, trade – giving up something to get something else – assumes scarcity. Resources are scarce wherever the desires of all persons for goods or services cannot be met. Hunger, in other words, is written into the conditions under which economics operates. There is never enough to go around. But it is not simply the hunger of those who lack sufficient food to keep their bodies in good health. Scarcity is the more general hunger of those who want more, without reference to what they already have. Economics will always be the science of scarcity as long as individuals continue to want. And we are told that human desires are endless.

This insight about desire is not new. For Augustine of Hippo the constant renewing of desire is a condition of being creatures in time. Desire is not simply negative; our desires are what get us out of bed in the morning. We desire because we live. The problem is that our desires continue to light on objects which fail to satisfy, objects on the lower end of the scale of being which, if cut off from the source of their being, quickly dissolve into nothing.[1] The solution to the restlessness of desire is to cultivate a desire for God, the eternal. Augustine famously prays to God that 'our heart is restless until it rests in you'.[2]

In a consumer-driven market economy, the restlessness of desire is also recognized. Marketing constantly seeks to meet, create, and stoke new desires, often by highlighting a sense of dissatisfaction with what one presently has and is. In a consumer culture, we recognize the validity of Augustine's insight: particular material things cannot satisfy. Rather than causing us to turn away from material things and towards God, however, in consumer culture we plunge ever more deeply into the world of things. Dissatisfaction and fulfillment cease to be opposites, for pleasure is not in possessing objects but in their pursuit. Possession kills *eros;* familiarity breeds contempt. This is why shopping itself has taken on the honored status of an addiction in Western society. It is not the desire for any thing in particular, but the pleasure of stoking desire itself that makes malls into the new cathedrals of Western culture. The dynamic is not an inordinate attachment to material things, but an irony and detachment from all things. At the level of economics, scarcity is treated as a tragic inability to meet the needs of all people, especially those whom hunger and extreme deprivation confront daily with death. At the level of experience, scarcity in consumer culture is associated with the pleasurable sensation of desiring. Scarcity is implied in the daily erotics of desire that keeps the individual in pursuit of novelty.

For a number of reasons, desire in consumer society keeps us distracted from the desires of the truly hungry, those who experience hunger as life-threatening deprivation. It is not simply that the market encourages an erotic attraction toward things, not persons. It is that the market story establishes a fundamentally individualistic view of the human person. The idea of scarcity assumes that the normal condition for the communication of goods is by trade. To get something, one must relinquish something else. The idea of scarcity implies that goods are not held in common. The consumption of goods is essentially a private experience. This does not mean that charitable giving is forbidden, but it is relegated to the private realm of preference, not justice. One might always send a check to help feed the hungry. One's charitable preferences however will always be in competition with one's own endless desires. The idea of scarcity establishes the view that *no-one* has enough. My desires to feed the hungry are always being distracted by the competition between their desires and my own.

Adam Smith thought that this distraction was a result of the fact that every person is 'by nature, first and principally recommended to his own care.'[3]

> Men, though naturally sympathetic, feel so little for another, with whom they have no particular connexion, in comparison of what they feel for themselves; the misery of one, who is merely their fellow-creature, is of so little importance to them in comparison even of a small conveniency of their own.[4]

In his *Theory of Moral Sentiments* Smith pondered the question of how disinterested moral judgments could ever trump self-interest. He developed the idea that pain and other sentiments are communicable from one individual to another by the ability of the human person sympathetically to put him or herself in the position of another. Nevertheless, according to Smith, nature has made our resentment to a lack of justice greater than our resentment to a lack of benevolence, so only the former is subject to punishment: 'when a man shuts his breast against compassion, and refuses to relieve the misery of his fellow-creatures, when he can with the greatest ease . . . though every body blames the conduct, nobody imagines that those who might have reason, perhaps, to expect more kindness, have any right to extort it by force.'[5] Society can exist without benevolence, but not without justice.[6] Absent explicit violence or theft, the inability of a person to feed him or herself is not a failure of justice, but a call for benevolence, which falls to individuals. The communicability of pain in the body of society is faint. Moral indignation in its strong form is reserved for explicit attacks on the status quo of life and property.

Adam Smith does not simply leave the care of the hungry to individual preference, however, for in the larger scheme of *The Wealth of Nations*, the needs of the hungry are addressed by the providential care of the market. According to Smith, the invisible hand of the market guides economic activity such that the pursuit of self-interest by uncoordinated individuals miraculously works out to the benefit of all. The great economic machine of society is driven by people's wants. Through the mechanism of demand and supply, the competition of self-interested individuals will result in the production of the goods society wants, at the right prices, with sufficient employment for all at the right wages for the foreseeable future. The result is an eschatology in which abundance for all is just around the corner. In the contemporary consumer-driven economy, consumption is often urged as the solution to the suffering of others. Buy more to get the economy moving – more consumption means more jobs. By the miracle of the market, my consumption feeds you. One story the market tells, then, is that of scarcity miraculously turned into abundance by consumption itself, a contemporary loaves-and-fishes saga.

In reality however consumerism is the death of Christian eschatology. There can be no rupture with the status quo, no inbreaking Kingdom of God, but only endless superficial novelty. Vincent Miller writes: 'Since desire is sustained by being detached from particular objects, consumer anticipation wishes for everything and hopes for nothing.'[7] The witness of the martyrs to living the Kingdom of God in the present becomes a curiosity; how could someone be so committed to some particular thing as to lose their life for it? We are moved by the suffering of others, but we can hardly imagine a change radical enough to undermine the paradigm of consumption. Even the suffering of others can become a spectacle and a consumable item[8] – tsunamis sell newspapers. And so we choose to believe that, through the miracle of free competition, our consumption will feed others. The truth however is that self-interested consumption does not bring justice to the hungry. The consumer's pursuit of low, low prices at Wal-Mart means low, low wages for the people in Asia who make the products we buy. Eschatological hope easily fades into resignation to a tragic world of scarcity.

II. Hunger and the Eucharist

The Eucharist tells another story about hunger and consumption. It does not begin with scarcity, but with the one who came that we might have life, and have it abundantly (John 10.10). Jesus said to them, 'I am the bread of life. Whoever comes to me will never be hungry.' (John 6.35). The insatiability of human desire is absorbed by the abundance of God's grace in the gift of the body and blood of Christ. 'Those who eat my flesh and drink my blood have eternal life' (6.54), they are raised above mere temporal longing for novelty. And the body and blood of Christ are not scarce commodities; the host and the cup are multiplied daily at thousands of Eucharistic celebrations throughout the world. 'Everything that the Father gives me will come to me, and anyone who comes to me I will never drive away.' (6.37)

This invitation to come and be filled can be assimilated to private spiritualities of self-fulfillment if it is packaged as an 'experience' of divine life. But the abundance of the Eucharist is inseparable from the *kenosis*, the self-emptying, of the cross. The consumer of the body and blood of Christ does not remain detached from what he or she consumes, but becomes part of the Body. 'Those who eat my flesh and drink my blood abide in me, and I in them.' (6:56) The act of consumption of the Eucharist does not entail the appropriation of goods for private use, but rather being assimilated to a public body, the Body of Christ. Augustine hears the voice of God say 'I am the food of the fully grown; grow and you will feed on me. And you will not change me into you like the food your flesh eats, but you will be changed into me.'[9] The Eucharist effects a radical de-centering of the individual by incorporating the person into a larger body. In the process, the act of consumption is turned inside-out, such that the consumer is consumed.

When we consume the Eucharist, we become one with others, and share their fate. Paul asks the Corinthians 'The bread that we break, is it not a sharing in the body of Christ?' Paul answers 'Because there is one bread, we who are many are one body, for we all partake of the one bread.' St. John Chrysostom comments on this passage:

> because he said A SHARING IN THE BODY, and that which shares is different from what it shares in, he removed even this small difference. For after he said A SHARING IN THE BODY, he sought again to express it more precisely, and so he added FOR WE, THOUGH MANY, ARE ONE BREAD, ONE BODY. 'For why am I speaking of sharing?' he says, 'We are that very body.' For what is the bread? The body of Christ. And what do they become who partake of it? The body of Christ; not many bodies, but one body.[10]

The enacting of the Body of Christ in the Eucharist has a dramatic effect on the communicability of pain from one person to another, for individuals are now united in one body, connected by one nervous system. Not only can the eye not say to the hand 'I have no need of you.' (1 Corinthians 12.21), but the eye and the hand suffer or rejoice in the same fate. 'If one member suffers, all suffer together with it; if one member is honored, all rejoice together with it.' (12.26). For this reason, Paul tells the Corinthians that we should take special care for the weakest members of the body (12.22–25), presumably because the whole body is only as strong as its weakest member.

This communicability of pain underlies the obligation of the followers of Christ toward the hungry. The point of the story of final judgment in Matthew 25.31–46 is not simply that an individual performing good deeds — such as feeding the hungry — will be rewarded with a ticket to the Kingdom. The force of the story lies in the identification of Christ with the hungry: 'for *I* was hungry and you gave me food' (25.35). The pain of the hungry person is the pain of Christ, and it is therefore also the pain of the member of Christ's body who feeds the hungry person. Unlike in Adam Smith, there is no priority of justice to charity here, no prior sorting out of who deserves what before benevolence can take place. In Matthew as in Paul, the hungry and the benevolent are confused in Christ, such that distinctions between justice and charity, public and private, become impediments to seeing reality as God sees it.

Adam Smith's economy underwrites a separation between contractual exchanges and gifts. Benevolence is a free suspension of self-interested exchange. As such, benevolence cannot be expected or even encouraged on the public level, because the market functions for the good of all on the basis of self-interested consumption and production. Benevolent giving freely transfers property from one to another, but nevertheless respects the boundaries between what is mine and what is yours. In the eucharistic economy, by contrast, the gift relativizes the boundaries between what is mine and what is yours by relativizing the boundary between me and you. We are no longer two individuals encountering each other either by way of contract or as active giver and passive recipient. Without losing our identities as unique persons – Paul's analogy of the body extols the diversity of eyes and hands, heads and feet – we cease to be merely other to one another by incorporation into the Body of Christ. In the Eucharist, Christ is gift, giver, and recipient. We are neither merely active nor passive, but participate in the divine life, such that we are fed and simultaneously become food for others.

Our temptation is to spiritualize all this talk of union, to make our connection to the hungry a mystical act of imaginative sympathy. We could then imagine that we are already in communion with those who lack food, whether or not we meet their needs. Matthew is having none of this, placing of the obligation to feed the hungry in the context of eschatological judgment. Paul too places neglect of the hungry in the context of judgment. At the Eucharistic celebration in Corinth, which included a common meal, those who eat while others go hungry 'show contempt for the church of God and humiliate those who have nothing' (1 Corinthians 11.22). Those who thus, in an 'unworthy manner', partake of the body and blood of Christ 'eat and drink judgment against themselves' (11.27.29). Those of us who partake in the Eucharist while ignoring the hungry may be eating and drinking our own damnation.

The Eucharist places judgment in the eschatological context of God's inbreaking Kingdom. Christian eschatology is not – as it is in Adam Smith — a gradual immanent progress toward abundance whereby the invisible hand of the market, operating through our consumption, promises an abundance for all that is always just a few years away. By contrast, the Eucharist announces the coming of the Kingdom of God now, already in the present, by the grace of God. Vatican II's *Sacrosanctum Concilium* affirms the eschatological dimension of the Eucharist in these terms: 'In the earthly liturgy we take part in a foretaste of that heavenly liturgy which is celebrated in the Holy City of Jerusalem toward which we journey as pilgrims . . .'[11] In the Eucharist, God breaks in and disrupts the tragic despair of human history with a message of hope and a demand for justice. The hungry cannot wait; the heavenly feast is now. The end-less consumption of superficial novelty is broken by the promise of an end, the Kingdom toward which history is moving and which is already breaking into history. The Kingdom is not driven by our desires but by God's desire which we receive as gift in the Eucharist.

I think I have an idea now of why it would have been wrong to give Rosalinda money for the bird. It would have annulled the gift and turned it into an exchange. It would have re-established the boundaries between what is hers and what is mine, and therefore reinforced the boundaries between her and me. The Eucharist tells a different story about who we — the hungry and the filled — really are, and where we are going.

Notes

1. Augustine, *Confessions*, trans. Henry Chadwick, Oxford, Oxford University Press, 1991, pp. 29–30 [Book II, §10].
2. Ibid., 3 [Book I, §1].
3. Adam Smith, *The Theory of Moral Sentiments*, edited by A.L. Macfie and D. D. Raphael, Oxford, Oxford University Press, 1976, p. 82 [II.ii.2.1].
4. Ibid., 86 [II.ii.3.4].
5. Ibid., 81 [II.ii.1.7].
6. Ibid., 85–91 [II.ii.3].
7. Vincent J. Miller, *Consuming Religion: Christian Faith and Practice in a Consumer Culture*, New York, Continuum, 2003, p. 132.
8. See ibid., 133–4.

9. Augustine, 124 [Book VII, §16].

10. St. John Chrysostom, 'Homily on I Corinthians, no. 24' in *The Eucharist: Message of the Fathers of the Church*, edited by Daniel J. Sheerin, Wilmington, Del., Michael Glazier, 1986), p. 210.

11. *Sacrosanctum Concilium* 8, in *Documents of Vatican II* edited by Austin P. Flannery, Grand Rapids, Mich., Wm. B. Eerdmans Publishing Co., 1975, p. 5.

Alms, Fasting, and Prayer:
The Work or Circle of Mercy and Adoration

LUIZ CARLOS SUSIN

Hunger, deprivation, bread, and word all have a deep mutual complicity. In the midst of temptation, Jesus moves from hunger for bread to hunger for the word: 'One does not live by bread alone, but by every word that comes from the mouth of God' (Matthew 4.4; cf Deuteronomy 8.2–3). But Jesus would have been familiar with the Jewish proverb: 'The one who eats is the most righteous of all' – righteous and pacified, satisfied, puffed up with righteousness – whereas the primordial emptiness from lack of food – hunger – places everyone in fear and danger, even making them dangerous and violent. Nonetheless, hunger and vulnerability, fear, shame, and compassion can set in motion a one-way course, an adventure in incarnation and animation, a spirituality continually deepened in withholding and excess of help for the body losing itself alone.[1] Jesus, with his helping actions, well knew the clamour of stomach and body that was physical hunger. He relieved the hungry crowd, in the most repeated and detailed action of his mission.

The hunger of others and his compassion for those who went around hungry also led Jesus to the most recurrent temptation, from the initial setting of his mission, travelling through the desert of his people and also in the closest and most everyday relationship with his people, who sought him because they wanted to eat and wanted to be sure of their food, to the point of making him the administrator and guarantor of their bread. If this was an obsessive temptation for him, this was because it remained on his missionary horizon as something that seemed good, that had something good about it, something viscerally good. Faced with this, seized with the giddiness of the hunger of those who sought him, Jesus was in need of discernment. But discernment means 'going to the heart', cutting through the shadows that threaten distractions, so that the very reality of temptation can become the source of the light of full truth that appears in it as dark truth, hidden in the depths of its shadows. In this case, this also involves the truth of his mission concerning something very basic: hunger, bread, word, prayer – that is, the glorification of God in living human beings, as in Irenaeus' saying, 'The glory of God is the living human being, and the glory of human beings is the vision of God.'

In Matthew's Gospel, in the programmatic words of the Sermon on the Mount, Jesus takes up and provides his slant on a traditional subject, the origin of which goes back to the dawn of religions: the practice of almsgiving, fasting, and prayer. This is a practice that persists in all religions as a form of piety and mercy. Still today, in Jerusalem on the Sabbath, those who come to the old city to pray by the mosques on the Temple Mount find, as they come through the gates in the walls, men, women, and children, some elegantly dressed in festive clothes, positioned next to the old arcades and taking up the traditional poses of beggars, with heads bowed, lips murmuring, cupped hands held out, sitting or stooping in a posture of humility. They are not necessarily poorer or more needy than the passers-by. This forms part of a ritual in which begging fulfils a function, almost doing a favour, for those going to the temple to pray: prayer supposes almsgiving and fasting; that is, giving something or being deprived of something. Without almsgiving and fasting, prayer is not deep and true but a pretence.

In the Sermon on the Mount, Jesus goes to the heart of giving and deprivation, even to the lonely extreme of one hand not knowing what the other is doing, and of shutting oneself in a room to pray, so that no one will know what is happening in the secrecy of the room in which prayer is being raised (cf Matthew 6.1–6). Therefore such radically giving and self-denying goodness is to be found with no sounding of trumpets or even self-awareness, without even the doer knowing there is goodness in his/her act of piety and mercy: the pure act of giving is that in which one hand does not know what the other is doing – the truly good is what *does not even know that it is good*.

At this time when the world's inequalities seem to be out of control, with symptoms of obesity a virtual epidemic on one hand and the violence generated by cynicism and revolt on another, it is worth reconsidering the 'threefold work of mercy' that goes with any truly religious approach, in which spirituality and materiality are called mutually to account and to shake hands in unification of the three basic religious gestures: almsgiving, fasting, and prayer.

I. 'Almsgiving' – or the holiness of giving

Let us take almsgiving first, though this order is methodological and peda-
gogical, since the three actions or moments – of giving, of fasting, and of
praying – form a circle, like that formed by the 'Three Graces' in Greek and
Roman tradition. Each one leads to the other, each one implies the other, is
'perichoretically' with the other, in the other, for the other, as is said of the
three Persons of the Trinity. Nevertheless, choosing this starting-point –
almsgiving – has a religious logic that will perhaps be seen as entirely clear
and necessary (perhaps more from the divine than the human viewpoint)
only at the end, together with the highest form of prayer – the purest thanksgiving, adoration. Another analogy can help us: knowledge of the Trinity
also necessarily starts from the humility of Jesus, the Son in human form, to
immerse itself finally in the ultimate mystery of the Father.

Almsgiving,[2] *eleemosyne* in Greek, derives from the root *éleos*, a Greek
word that, according to Bultmann, in classical literature denotes 'the distur-
bance occasioned by the sight of a harm afflicting another person', which
produces compassion and piety. It is a feeling of *pain at another's pain* and so
the opposite of envy, which is pain at another's wellbeing, and the opposite
of rejoicing at another's misfortune or suffering. The Greek Bible uses *éleos*
to translate the Hebrew *hesed*, one of the commonest adjectives used –
around four hundred times in the scriptures – to qualify God's manner of
being, and therefore a divine attribute of the first magnitude: indulgence,
generosity, goodness, friendship and faithfulness – essential elements of
God's compassionate and merciful dealings. In its simplest and most direct
form it is translated as 'mercy'. But it also corresponds to the Hebrew word
tsedaqah, the justice and measure appropriate in view of the fragile condition
of creatures. This is not a question of retributive justice, the 'measure' of the
classic Aristotelian and Roman maxim, 'Give to each what is his' – *Unicuique
suum*. It is, rather, 'creative justice', generous and generative, which exceeds
measures and creates a new situation, one of life, where before there was a
situation of deprivation with the threat of death. This is how to understand
Bultmann's statement, 'We are all God's beggars', indebted to God's mercy,
rescued and justified by God's piety.

We are, though, also one another's beggars. The sociology and anthropology of Émile Durkheim and above all of Marcel Mauss, as expressed
fundamentally in his *Essai sur le don* of 1924, showed that offerings, the rules
of giving, formed traditional societies and established them in a sphere of
sacrality in which what was secular could not be separated from what was

religious: all social activity, including economic activity, was regulated by relationships of giving and was founded on a basically religious approach to giving, which embraced and inspired economic activity.

It is openly secularized modern society that has unreservedly elevated individualism – 'anti-gift' – to a common principle, shared by all and therefore 'sacred', uniting everyone 'religiously' in a consensus around the sacrality of the individual and moulding society on a powerful yet socially destructive basic principle – individualism, which 'does not share'. Because it does not share its being, it does not share its possessions or its power. The pessimism of these anthropologists, to which must be added the famous pessimism of Lévy-Strauss, with regard to the future of individualist and capitalist Western society, means that they are describing – strictly speaking, etymologically – a 'diabolic religion'.

Nevertheless, despite everything that can and should be criticized in our dominant Western culture – individualist, capitalist, mercantilist, in which 'to each his own' works as a dynamic form of exploitation and appropriation on the basis of what is one's own, and where society's paradigms seem to oscillate brazenly between the 'individualism' that has no eyes or heart for others and a 'collectivism' that submits the public sphere to the State, treating individuals as a mass – there is still a *tertium non datur* – a 'third paradigm', today also called a 'third sector' – which in fact shows something deeper than and antecedent to the apparently iron dialectic between individual and collective: the 'paradigm of gift'. The Anti-Utilitarian Movement in Social Sciences (whose acronym, MAUSS, for the French *Mouvement anti-utilitariste en sciences sociales*, refers to Marcel Mauss, who inspired the movement) endeavours to show how the paradigm of gift lies at the very root of the modern secularized market and affirmation of individuals.[3] A very simple example is the way the cycle of annual feasts with the attendant need to give presents affects the market by stimulating sales and purchases. The ultimate purpose of this whole movement does not end with exchanging gifts but in the human need to create bonds, to establish and strengthen sacred alliances, on which, in the final analysis, society and the self-affirmation of individuals both rest. In its most dramatic version, this logic can be seen in a billboard strategically placed by an NGO in Candelária, Rio de Janeiro, at the spot that had been the scene of a multiple murder of street children by the police, proclaiming: 'Help those in need today so you don't become their victim tomorrow'.

Gifts, offerings, investments with no return for the investors: these are the basis of the justice sought not only in primary family relationships, where parents invest unilaterally in their children, but also in innumerable philanthropic initiatives, in NGOs, in social movements, in popular organizations. There is an infinite variety of forms of voluntary work, of aid, of adjustment of the means of exchange, which show the permanence and the pervasiveness of the 'gift paradigm' underlying market and state paradigms.

In the age of Keynesian economic and political theory, which gave rise to the Welfare State, the State was increasingly endowed with the role of provider, the provident State, to the point where its relationship with its citizens was governed by an ever more all-embracing web of their rights and its duties. As the figure of the 'public benefactor' faded – the relatively powerful local personage who combined his enterprises with the common good and ended with a statue in the town square or a street named after him – so the State's duties and the rights and expectations of citizens increased. The public sphere became inflated to such an extent that it has finally 'gone bankrupt' in a sense, or is at least being diminished or dismantled, reduced to 'little government' – dangerously little – with the market and private initiatives, whose basic ideology follows the ideology of individualism in investments and profits, once again called on to occupy the sphere previously considered public and the State's responsibility.

Today we are faced with the 'public-private partnership', involving privatization of the most basic services that should be ordered to the good of all, moving public services from direct state provision to private business intermediaries, involving the market and private finance initiatives in social matters, or a mixture of the two, in a somewhat confused way still dependent on goodwill. Many enterprises wishing to appear 'politically correct' and to make a favourable impression on potential clients associate their 'mission' with social benefits and campaigns. But there are also considerable doses of sincere quest for solutions to social problems. In Brazil, 'Zero Hunger' has perhaps become a good example of the realization that all authorities in a society need to take basic account of the fact that it will not survive unless it rests on the 'gift paradigm'. The general call to action, besides mobilizing state and business powers, naturally includes the churches among those who act as a 'third sector', since it is absolutely natural for religious activity and the gift paradigm to have an intrinsic mutual alliance. And for our present considerations, this is intrinsically biblical and evangelical.

In biblical terms, suffice to recall the institution of the Sabbath and the Jubilee. These have a theological grounding in the act of creation: the Creator resting in his creatures. But they also bring social measures: all creatures, including beasts of burden – not just the birds of the air – as well as all human beings, be they children or slaves, should have the right to rest, to eat, and to have secure land tenure. The passing of time brings unevenness, increasing deprivations for some and gains for others. Then measures laid down for the Sabbath and the Jubilee become necessary. Only in this way can we dream of an earth brought to the fullness of the eschatological Sabbath, to its rest with its Creator.[4]

Jesus, by insisting on giving, on generosity, on mercy, on creative justice and not simply retributive justice – giving only to those who give, healing only those who heal us, or even paying each worker rigorously according to hours worked and production achieved (cf Matthew 20.1–16) – breaks with the harsh line of the law, as he does with ritual as the practice of religion. The result of this is, for example, James' synthesis of true religion, 'pure and undefiled': caring for orphans and widows (James 1.27).

Jesus gives us a fabulous example of a particular widow, recalled through Luke's sensitivity: she, by giving 'two small copper coins' from her poverty gives more than the riches contributed by those who enjoy fame and status from their overabundance. The widow here is the gift paradigm to which we aspire: 'Truly I tell you, this poor widow has put in more than all of them; for all of them have contributed out of their abundance, but she out of her poverty has put in all she had to live on' (Luke 21.3–4). This is the true almsgiving, mercy that is beyond measure, whose generosity wrests our very vitals from ourselves, sheltering and nourishing others at the expense of our own lives: the gift of what means life itself, and so not what is superfluous but what is necessary, what is going to remedy a lack, a loss, a fast.

II. From almsgiving to fasting from essentials

The widow, out of her poverty, gave what she had to live on – all she possessed. By depriving herself of what she offered, she reduced herself to even greater poverty, the threatening penury of hunger and lack of means necessary to satisfy her wants. She redirected her 'portion', what would be sufficient to put in her mouth to quell her hunger, her 'just measure'; she took this out of her mouth in order to offer it to those who would, according to custom, be helped by the temple alms. It was the mouth, the stomach, and the starving body of the poor that challenged and took away the little she had. She was a defenceless woman by reason of her widowhood, and she risked more than reasonable prudence would have dictated. She certainly reasoned with her maternal stomach, with the groans for mercy from the stomach she sought to protect and nourish. But she did this at the expense of herself, of her hunger, of her mouth with no mouthful, making herself stay dangerously famished, fasting from what was essential to her body.

Fasting takes many forms and has many goals, with therapeutic and aesthetic results acting as widespread incentives today. The widow in the gospel, however, leads us, plunges us, into the biblical and theological meaning of fasting, as Isaiah dramatically describes:

'Why do we fast, but you do not see?
Why humble ourselves, but you do not notice?'
Look, you serve your own interest on your fast day,
and oppress all your workers.
Look, you fast only to quarrel and to fight
 and to strike with a wicked fist.
Such fasting as you do today
will not make your voice heard on high. [. . .]
Is not this the fast that I choose:
to loose the bonds of injustice.
to undo the thongs of the yoke,
to let the oppressed go free,
and to break every yoke?
Is it not to share your bread with the hungry,
and bring the homeless poor into your house;
when you see the naked, to cover them,
and not to hide yourself from your own kin?
Then your light shall break forth like the dawn,
and your healing shall spring up quickly. [. . .]
Then you shall call, and the LORD will answer;
you shall cry for help, and he will say, Here I am.

(Isa. 58.3–4, 6, 8, 9)

Fasting here is the outcome of giving, of caring, of mercy, of hunger, and of the struggle for justice. The widow in Luke 21, like the widow of Naim in his 7.11ff, vividly recalls the widow of Zarephath, who helped Elijah at the expense of herself and her son, risking shortening their lives in order to share the morsel of meal she had with this stranger and unwelcome guest (cf 1 Kings 17.8–24).

The gospels also show us a fasting associated with the gift of time, and today this is most significant in mutual support among the poor, who, having nothing else to give, offer their most precious good: time. When Jesus invites his disciples to 'rest a while', the evangelist makes the detailed observation that 'so many were coming and going, and they had no leisure even to eat' (Mark 6.31). This, gradually building up, is the most complete of various observations made by Mark, since the pressure on Jesus began early, shortly after his first preaching in Capharnaum, when Simon and his companions tell him that 'Everyone is searching for you', interrupting his prayer and themselves hunting anxiously for him and concerned for their own positions of power (cf Mark 1.35ff). It is the verb 'hunt' (or at least 'look for') that will be used to pursue and justify Jesus' death (cf Mark 14.55). Back in Capharnaum some days later, 'So many gathered around that there was no longer room for them, not even in front of the door' (Mark 2.2). When he went home, 'the crowd came together again, so that they could not even eat. When his family heard it, they went out to restrain him, for people were saying, "He has gone out of his mind"' (Mark 3.20–21). Here, then, is fasting as a result of missionary commitment, which includes the gift of that most precious commodity, time.

III. From fasting from essentials to substantive prayer

In fasting from essentials, the fasting of the widow, of the missionary among the poor, a fast not chosen but forced by the wound of mercy; in the gift of what is absolutely necessary, the 'mouthful' painfully diverted from one's own mouth to nourish and satisfy the mouths of the starving, their very lack and hunger makes those who fast 'all mouth' for God's hunger. This is the fasting that leads to the most steadfast and substantive prayer. This is not fasting for one's health or in preparation for more concentrated prayer in an *alpha* state of mind. Quite the contrary: this fasting is 'to one's own detriment' through being overwhelmed by others, through having to nourish and care for others, a fairly everyday experience for mothers caring for families.

Time taken away through many preoccupations and concerns with the needs of others, a heart emptied by feelings of mercy, a stomach gripped with hunger from having its mouthful given away: these 'sincerely' open one's mouth – bringing one's heart into one's mouth – for being fed with the bread that satisfies and gives meaning to the heart's hunger: the Word of God. Only those who have been through the radical despoiling of self-giving through giving what was most needed and just for them – their mouthful, their ration, their right – are engaged in the fasting that becomes all mouth, like fledglings in a nest facing the parent bird bringing them food, so that they can be fed by the Word of God. This is the ad-oration that is pleasing to God. Ad-oration, etymologically, means turning one's mouth toward what promises nutrition, toward what is capable of filling one's mouth and satisfying one's empty heart. Adoration in Lacanesque and post-modern terms might perhaps be the 'longing' excavated from the void, from lack, from precariousnes. This is how we might understand the evangelical assertion at the head of this article: 'One does not live by bread alone, but by every word that comes from the mouth of God' (Matthew 4.4).

Now the word comes from 'the mouth of God'. In some sense, then, God himself, in opening his mouth to give his word, empties himself, renounces keeping for himself the food that is in his heart – and 'the Word became flesh' (John 1.14). How scandalous, how humble, and how poor is the manner in which God approaches to nourish those who hunger for God! God feeds the void and the hunger of those fasting who open their mouths with his own divine self-emptying and with his fragility as a starving God – identified with 'the least of' those who hunger (cf Isaiah 57.15; Matthew 25.40, 45). Paul categorically states this mystery, while recounting his initiative in making a collection for the needy of Palestine, as an exchange of generosities, of gifts, of assistance to the poverty of both parties, Greeks and Palestinians: 'For you know the generous act of our Lord Jesus Christ, that though he was rich, yet for your sakes he became poor, so that by his poverty you might become rich' (2 Corinthians 8.9). So it is from the poverty – the lack or longing – of the Son of God, and not from riches that those who fast and long are fed. It is God's void and longing that value and say to those who fast in the hope of being fed from the mouth of God, 'I love you'. A meeting of voids and longings, of mutual loving. A still deeper lack, a still more intense longing, a still more intense quest: such is the movement that leads to adoration and is the highest homage to God and the most subtle and paradoxical presence of God: merciful, supportive, comforting, and consoling in his Word that makes the whole process – almsgiving, fasting, prayer – into a *process of the very God and of affiliation to God's mode of being.* The first who loved, who gave the essential alms – God's gift of his beloved Son –and fasts in his Son and ad-ores us and wants to see us coming to our meeting in his Son, is God himself. In order to come close to God, we are endowed with the same method and pedagogy of self-emptying and loving.

In this way we learn that we are saved from the materiality of our bodies, from our hunger and our search for bread for ourselves, through the spirituality that begins in vulnerability to the hunger and to the bodies of others, to the search for bread for others, beginning with the gift of the mouthful from our own mouth. We are thereby also saved from the narcissism of fasting and from the illusion of prayer, since only the mouth of God, God's given and despoiled Word, can sustain a fast imposed by the excessive giving provoked by others who hunger.

Within this overflowing of mercy we also find the just measure for caring for ourselves, for taking care of our hunger, our bodies, and our bread, with the right to rest in anticipation of the Sabbath, of festival and rejoicing. This is how we should understand Jesus, according to Luke, after so many meals shared with generous –even scandalous –hospitality:

> When the hour came, he took his place at the table, and the apostles with him. He said to them, 'I have eagerly desired to eat this Passover with you before I suffer; for I tell you, I will not eat it until it is fulfilled in the king-dom of God. [. . .] You are those who have stood by me in my trials; and I confer on you, just as my Father has conferred on me, a kingdom, so that you may eat and drink at my table in my kingdom' (Luke 22.4–16, 28–30).

Let us end by paraphrasing Teresa and John of the Cross – 'love is paid with love' – saying of God that 'hunger is repaid with more hunger', as is 'longing with still more ardent longing', once what we most long for from others, in love, in longing for their word and presence, is longing for them to long for us, to offer us their longing, to make us what they long for, so that our lack is fulfilled in the lack of us they suffer. And in this co-suffering hunger and fasting between the Creator and his creatures, between the Father and his children, we find the words, the ad-orations, the hospitality of the Kingdom, 'the food that endures for eternal life (John 6.27b).

Translated by Paul Burns

Notes

1. I owe much of what I develop here, focussed on Jesus, to the great Jewish philosopher and teacher Emanuel Levinas whose thought was the subject of my doctoral thesis. He repeatedly returned to the drama of hunger, of the body, of bread, as the ethical and basic challenges of a real spirituality of thanksgiving. See documented synthesis in L. C. Susin, *O Homen messiânico: Uma introducão ao pensamento de Emmanuel Levinas*, Porto Alegre 1984, pp. 345–50.
2. Cf H.-H. Eser, 'Misericórdia', in L. Coen, E. Beyreuther, and H. Bietenhard (eds), *Dizionario dei concetti biblici del Nuovo Testamento*, Bologna 1976, pp. 1013–18.

3. References to the 'gift paradigm' and MAUSS include A. Caillé, *Anthropologie du don*, Paris 2000; P. H. Martins (ed.), *A dádiva entre os modernos*, Petrópolis 2002; J. T. Godbout, *L'esprit du don*, Paris 1992; M. Mauss, *The Gift*, London 1925.

4. On the theology of the Jubilee Year and the Sabbath see L. C. Susin, 'Cristo senhor do Sábado', *Convergencia* 35, no. 337 (2000), pp. 543–50.

Contributors

FREI BETTO (Carlos Alberto Libânio Christo) is a Dominican friar, journalist and writer, militant and adviser on social movements and pastoral strategies. His book *Batismo de Sangue* (Baptism of Blood), in which he narrates his actions and imprisonment during the time of military dictatorship in Brazil, in the 1960s and 1970s, won the nation's major literary prize, the Jabuti, in 1985. His many works include the christological essays *Entre todos os homens* and *A obra do artista: uma visão holística do Universo*. In 2003–4 he acted as special adviser to President Lula and co-ordinator of the Zero Hunger social mobilization campaign. He contributes to numerous journals and reviews.

E-mail: fbetto@uol.com.br

CHRISTOPHE BOUREUX OP was born in France in 1958. He gained a doctorate in theology and religious anthropology in 1994 and now teaches in the theological faculty of the Institute Catholique de Lille. For fifteen years he has been responsible for training young Dominicans in northern France. He is the author of *Les plantes de la Bible et leur symbolique*, Paris 2001.

Address: Couvent des dominicains, 7 Avenue Salomon, 59800 Lille, France. Email: cboureux@nordnet.fr

JOEL MARIE CABRITA was born in Zimbabwe and lived in Swaziland from the ages of two to eighteen. After completing a degree in Theology at Cambridge University she taught high school in Swaziland and worked for an HIV-AIDS charity. She then did a Masters in Philosophical Theology at the University of Virginia and is now writing a doctoral thesis at Cambridge on the topic of 'descriptive' theology with reference to religious identity in South Africa.

Address: Trinity College, Cambridge, CB2 1TQ, UK.

WILLIAM T. CAVANAUGH is Associate Professor of Religion at the University of St Thomas, St Paul, MN. His publications include *Theopolitical Imagination: Discovering the Liturgy as a Political Act in an Age of Global Consumerism* (Edinburgh: T. & T. Clark, 2002) and *Torture and Eucharist: Theology, Politics, and the Body of Christ* (Oxford: Blackwell Publishers, 1998).

Address: Dept of Theology, University of St. Thomas, 2115 Summit Ave, St. Paul, MN, 55105, USA.

ROBERT DODARO is President and Professor of Patristics at the Patristic Institute, the Augustinianum, in Rome. He is the author of *Christ and the Just Society in the Thought of Augustine* (2004).

Address: Institutum Patristicum Augustinianum, Via Paolo VI, 25, I-00193 Italy.
Email: rdodaro@aug.org

ANNE FORTIN is professor of reflective theology at Laval University, Quebec. She also holds the Chair of Teaching and Research on Understanding Faith in the Modern Age, which aims to form priests and pastoral workers. Her fields of study are Christology and the Trinity, plus reading biblical texts and tradition from a semiotic viewpoint. Her more recent publications include 'Parler de Dieu et du Christ, un défi ecclésial pour la dogmatique', in *Laval théologique et philosophique* 60, no, 1 (Feb. 2004); 'Hommage a Raymond Lemieux: la Bible comme lettre d'amour volée', in A. Fortin and F. Nault (eds) *Dire l'impensable, l'Autre. Pérégrinations avec Rayond Lemieux* (2004); 'Faire circuler la parole', in G. Routhier and M. Viau (eds) *Précis de théologie pratique* (2004); 'Laisser parler la parole (Mc 2.2). Une pratique réglée du texte biblique au service de la vie de l'Église' in *Sémiotique et Bible* 115 (Sept. 2004).

Address: Faculté de théologie et de sciences religieuses, Université Laval, Québec, Québec G1K 7P4, Canada.
E-mail: Anne.Fortin@ftsr.ulaval.ca

ÉRICO HAMMES teaches graduate and post-graduate courses in theology at the Pontifical Catholic University of Rio Grande do Sul in Porto Alegre, Brazil. He holds a doctorate in systematic theology from the Gregoriana, with a thesis on the Christology of Jon Sobrino. Besides theology and Latin

American culture, he studies dialogue with other sciences and inter-religious dialogue in the fields of Christology and Trinitarian theology, as well as twentieth-century European theology, especially Bonhoeffer, Moltmann, and Rahner.

Address: FATEO-PUCRS, Av. Ipiranga 6681, 90619–900 Porto Alegre – RS, Brazil.
E-mail: ehammes@pucrs.br

ANGEL F. MENDEZ, OP, is a native of Mexico, and a Dominican friar in the Southern Dominican Province, USA. Before entering the Order of Preachers, he was a professional Modern/Contemporary dancer mainly dancing with professional companies in Mexico and the USA. He holds a BA in Dance, a BA in Philosophy, a MA in Theology and a MDiv. He is preparing a dissertation with the title 'Alimentation: Theology as a Culinary Art'.

Address: 2502 Comburg Castleway, Austin, TX 78748, USA.
E-mail: afm2b@cgatepro-2.mail.virginia.edu

HADWIG ANA MARIA MÜLLER is Consultant for Mission Processes in Europe at the Missionswissenschaftliches Institut Missio e.V. in Aix-en-Chapelle/ Germany.

Address: Missionswisschenschaftliches Institut Missio e.V., Goethestraße 43, 52064 Aachen, Germany.
E-Mail: mwi@mwi-aachen.org

LOUIS PANIER was born in Dole in the Jura region of France in 1945. He lectures in Semiotics in the department of linguistic science at the Lumière University of Lyon and is technical director of CADIR (the Centre for Analysis of Religious Discourse) at the theology department of the Catholic University of Lyon and of the review *Sémiotique et Bible*. Besides a number of collaborative works, his principal publications include *La naissance du Fils de Dieu. Sémiotique et Théologie discursive. Lecture de Luc 2* (1991), *Le péché Originel. Naissance de l'homme sauvé* (1996), and (as editor) *Les Lettres dans la Bible et dans la litérature* (1999).

Address: 5 avenue Pierre Mendès-France, CP11 – 69676 BRON CEDEX, France.
E-mail: louis.panier@univ-lyon2.fr

JANET MARTIN SOSKICE is the University Reader in Phiosophical Theology at the University of Cambridge, UK. She is a past president of the Catholic Theological Association of Great Britain and a member of the board of directors of *Concilium*.

Address: Faculty of Divinity, University of Cambridge, West Road, Cambridge, CB3 9BS, UK.
E-mail: j.soskice@jesus.cam.ac.uk

LUIS CARLOS SUSIN is a Cappuchin Friar who received a doctorate from the Pontifical University Gregoriana in Rome. He is professor at the PUC-RS and at the Ecola Superior de Teologia e Espiritualidade Franciscana (Estef) in Porto Alege. He is a member of the Board of Directors of Concilium and a founding member and former President of SOTER (Socialidade de Teologia e Ciências de Religião). He frequently teaches theology in Brazil and other countries. He is the author of several books including *A criação de Deus e Jesus, filho de Deus e filho de Maria*.

Address: Faculté de Théologie, Av. Ipiranga 6681, 90619-900, Porto Alegre (RS), Brazil

MARIE-THERES WACKER is Professor for Old Testament and Theological Women's Studies at the Roman Catholic Faculty of Theology of the University of Münster in Germany. She has published widely in the fields of feminist biblical exegesis, Jewish-Christian dialogue and the discussion about monotheism in Israel.

Address: Hüfferstraße 27, D-48149 Münster, Germany.
E-mail: femtheo@uni-muenster.de

The editors thank the following for their help in preparing this issue: Richard Cote, Virgil Elizondo, Anne Fortin, Rosino Gibellini, Michel de Goedt, Ottmar John, Maureen Junker-Kenny, Armidio Rizzi, Christoph Theobald, Andrés Torres Queiruga, Marie-Theres Wacker.

Concilium Subscription Information

February   2005/1: *Cyberspace – Cyberethics – Cybertheology*

April   2005/2: *Hunger, Bread and the Eucharist*

June   2005/3: *Christianity in Crisis*

October   2005/4: *A Forgotten Future: Vatican II*

December   2005/5: *Islam: New Issues*

New subscribers: to receive Concilium 2005 (five issues) anywhere in the world, please copy this form, complete it in block capitals and send it with your payment to the address below.

Please enter my subscription for *Concilium* 2005

Individuals   Institutions
____ £35.00 UK/Rest of World   ____ £48.50 UK/Rest of World
____ $67.00 North America   ____ $93.50 North America
____ €60.00   ____ €80.00.50

Please add £17.50/$33.50/€30 for airmail delivery

Payment Details:

Payment must accompany all orders and can be made by cheque or credit card
I enclose a cheque for £/$ _____ Payable to SCM-Canterbury Press Ltd
Please charge my Visa/MasterCard (Delete as appropriate) for £/$ _____
Credit card number ....
Expiry date ....
Signature of cardholder ....
Name on card ....
Telephone .... E-mail ....

Send your order to *Concilium*, SCM-Canterbury Press Ltd
9–17 St Albans Place, London N1 ONX, UK
Tel +44 (0)20 7359 8033 Fax +44 (0)20 7359 0049
E-Mail: office@scm-canterburypress.co.uk

Customer service information:
All orders must be prepaid. Subscriptions are entered on an annual basis (i.e. January to December) No refunds on subscriptions will be made after the first issue of the Journal has been despatched. If you have any queries or require information about other payment methods, please contact our Customer services department.

Breinigsville, PA USA
14 January 2011
253304BV00005B/1/P

9 780334 030836